TONY EVANS
KINGDOM FOCUS

FOCUS
ON THE FAMILY.

A Focus on the Family Resource
Published by Tyndale House Publishers

Kingdom Focus: Rethinking Today in Light of Eternity
© 2023 Tony Evans. All rights reserved.

A Focus on the Family book published by Tyndale House Publishers, Carol Stream, Illinois 60188

Cover design by Eva M. Winters

Cover photograph of Earth horizon copyright © James Thew/Adobe Stock. All rights reserved.

Cover photograph of stars by Wil Stewart on Unsplash.com.

For information about special discounts for bulk purchases, please contact Tyndale House Publishers at csresponse@tyndale.com, or call 1-855-277-9400.

ISBN 978-1-58997-952-9

Printed in the United States of America

29 28 27 26 25 24 23
7   6   5   4   3   2   1

CONTENTS

INTRODUCTION

A story is told about a young boy who lost his contact lens one day. As he was trying to put it in, he accidentally dropped the contact onto the floor of the bathroom. The young boy got down on his hands and knees, attempting to locate the unlocatable. After a few minutes, his mom walked in and saw what he was doing.

The boy told his mom what had happened. She knelt, looked around, and quickly spotted the contact. After she handed it to her son, the boy asked with a surprised look on his face, "How did you find it so fast? I've been looking for at least ten minutes!" His mom replied, "Oh, that's easy. You were looking for a contact. I was looking for $250. That makes a big difference!"

Your focus is often determined by your need. If the young boy never found the contact, he knew his mom would somehow find a way to replace it. But his mom knew that if *she* didn't locate the contact, she would be out their grocery money for the next week. This awareness of how critical it was to locate the contact heightened her ability to focus. As a result, she found exactly what she was looking for.

Focus makes just as much of a difference in your life and mine. If we are busy focusing on external frivolities or personal ambitions rather than on the kingdom of God, we wind up missing out on serving God's kingdom as well as the other things we had hoped to attain in life. How do I know? Jesus said just this. In Matthew 6:33, He stated it as plainly as anyone ever could: "But seek first His kingdom and His righteousness, and all these things will be provided to you."

We often rush over that verse since it is one so many of us are familiar with. I think it might have a greater impact if we were to invert it into the negative form instead: Do not seek first the kingdom of God and His righteousness, and you will not have many of the other things you desire either.

That's pretty clear. The psalmist said it in another way: "Delight yourself in the LORD; and He will give you the desires of your heart" (Psalm 37:4). If we invert that verse into the negative, it goes something like this: Do not delight yourself in the Lord, and He will not give you the desires of your heart. When you put it like that, it's easy to see where we need to place our attention in this life. Where we focus matters not only for eternity but—as seen from these two foundational verses—it also matters in our lives right now.

As we began to experience life returning to a more normal routine after the COVID-19 pandemic, I heard people comment on how the lockdowns and the pandemic season overall were personally clarifying for them. That time gave them the space they needed to see what really mattered to them. Many people moved across the country to be closer to family. Others changed jobs. Some people even changed careers entirely, and one family I know decided to retire early and move to the Caribbean. That specific season of space and change opened many eyes to what was truly important.

In Scripture, God tells us what means the most to Him. When we align our lives with His Word, we get to experience the greatest freedom we could ever know. We get to experience a life covered with His covenantal care. In this book, we are going to spend some time focusing on the things God Himself focuses on in Scripture. We are going to explore the issues that delight His heart so that we can discover the joy and the power of delighting in the same—or similar—things.

The first half of the book will examine the spiritual habits we can employ to sharpen our focus for His kingdom and fully maximize our lives while on earth. The second half of the book will take us deeper into the character and heart of God, and we'll see how His love for us guides us every step of the way. I've intentionally designed the book in this way so that we can start with the foundation and then build upon it with that which will produce the most fruit in our experience as kingdom followers on earth.

I'm grateful you've chosen to spend your time with me in these pages. I'm grateful because this area of living in view of God's overarching perspective is one that very few Christians grasp fully, yet it impacts our lives probably more than anything other than our salvation in Jesus Christ. My prayer for you as you travel through these chapters is that God will take the truths and principles in every paragraph and write them on your heart.

It is my hope that God will sharpen your focus, transform your mind, and empower you to live every aspect of your life in light of the kingdom to which you have been chosen and called, for such a time as this.

1

THE PURSUIT

One of my favorite areas of ministering over the years has been my ministry to professional athletes. Whether their sport is basketball, baseball, or football, I consider it an honor every time a player looks to me as a confidant, counselor, and friend. Everyone who knows me knows that I'm an avid sports enthusiast. I love the thrill of competition. I enjoy watching athletes push themselves further than they ever thought they could. I eat up the passion of the pursuit. Because of this, ministering to athletes and making an impact on their lives in whatever way I can has brought deep satisfaction to me.

One of the mindsets of professional athletes that I relate to the most involves their focus on working toward a goal. For example, every football player who goes to the NFL joins a team that has one overarching goal: not only to reach the Super Bowl at the end of the year but also to win it.

I've had the privilege of speaking to several NFL teams the night before the big Super Bowl game, and the collective energy in the room always astounds me. There is a synergized force generated when so many passionate, dedicated, and committed men come together in pursuit of a common goal. All eyes are on that one prize—the Lombardi Trophy.

In fact, all eyes were on that prize as far back as that season's summer practices. Or even as far back as college or high school. For many players, their eyes were on that prize when they were young kids playing football with their friends on a Saturday afternoon. Their focus didn't begin the night before the Super Bowl. No, these football players committed to focusing on the goal long before hard work and determination got them to the Super Bowl.

That focus was present in the gym, where repetition after repetition was made to tear down and build up muscle, and on the field, where play after play was run to fine-tune moves and skills. It was the focus on that goal that drove those men, goading them every painful and exhausting step of the way.

Without that goal, the effort would have waned.

Without that goal, the early-hour workouts would have been skipped from time to time.

Without that goal, passion would have eventually fizzled while partying took its place.

It is that one goal—to win the game that publicly declares that this team is the absolute greatest of the year—that prompts their continual pursuit. Winning the Super Bowl seals a team's place in history. It's the goal that drives these players, coaches, and support staff to work when no one is watching, to persevere when their muscles are aching and their eyes are weary from studying so much film.

You will never hear a single player or a single coach from any NFL team in the league say at the beginning of the season, "Well, I hope we win a game or two this year." Never. The goal is not to win a game or two. The goal isn't to win more games than last year. The goal isn't simply to improve the team's record, fill more stadium seats, or increase publicity. While these things are good for a football team, none of them is the true goal. The goal is the trophy, short and simple.

The goal is victory in the final game of the year.

The passionate pursuit of this goal governs the life of every teammate. It is this focus that dictates their diet, workout routines, sleep patterns, planning, and more. It is this drive that impacts everything. Every single decision converges toward the pursuit of winning the very last game of the year.

And while it doesn't take much of a stretch for us to understand, appreciate, or even respect this mindset of professional athletes, we often seem unable to understand why a similar degree of drive and passion ought to apply to us as followers of Jesus Christ.

As kingdom followers, you and I play on the same team. We play on God's kingdom team. As a result, we all share the same goal. We also play underneath the direction of the same coaching staff. And we have our own spiritual Super Bowl of sorts that we are working toward. Now, while the game itself does play out on earth, the ceremony and celebration for this final victory takes place in eternity.

It is possible that this disconnect—the gulf between what we do *here* and the ultimate results of it *there*—is what often divides our focus. The truth is that far too many of us fail to live our lives on earth with an eternal mindset. But whether we do or do not focus on eternity, the outcome is inevitable. One day you and I will stand before the judgment seat of Christ. We will transition from here to there, and we will stand before the Lord. And when we do, we will have one of two potential experiences.

The first option is to stand before Christ as a spiritual success and victor, having lived out His will on earth. The other option is to stand before Him, having failed to maximize the destiny He placed you here to pursue.

To gain His ultimate trophy is to hear the words "Well done, good and faithful servant" (Matthew 25:21, ESV). The alternative is to fail to receive a healthy measure of our eternal rewards. Which set of outcomes you experience is entirely dependent upon you. Your choices, thoughts, emotions, and effort on earth will define your eternal rewards. Eternity itself is secured through faith in Christ alone. But the level of rewards you get to experience is up to you.

Every Super Bowl has two opposing teams warring against each other for the trophy. Our spiritual pursuit looks a little different. It is you, the Christian, warring against the evil forces of Satan and his minions, as well as against your own sin nature. There is an important difference in this battle from what we see in a typical game. The forces you are fighting are not seeking the same prize that you are. Rather, they are intent on unseating you from gaining *your* prize.

It's like an NFL team that has already been eliminated from the playoffs but still plays to win its final games. The motivation for their victory lies in their desire to knock someone else out of the running to get what they can no longer have themselves. Satan no longer has a shot at an eternity marked with joy, goodness, or eternal rewards. His fate was sealed when he chose to rebel against God at the beginning of time. But that doesn't stop him from trying to keep us from gaining our eternal rewards.

And mark my words: Satan's strategy is shrewd.

He seeks to keep you living in a state of forgetfulness. He wants you to forget who you are in Christ. He wants you to forget that you belong to another King and another kingdom. He wants you to forget that earth is not really your home. It is by forgetting these things, and more, that you stop pursuing the rewards of that coming day. If Satan can erase the fact from your mind that you will one day stand before the judgment seat of Christ, he can stunt your progress in serving the kingdom on earth. If Satan can remove the thought of eternity from every item on your life's itinerary, then he will get you to live only for right now, for what you can see, feel, and experience in the moment.

When this happens, Satan not only cripples God's kingdom agenda from advancing on earth, but he also robs you from obtaining the full potential of your eternal reward. Satan is the thief who has come to "steal and kill and destroy" (John 10:10).

But God has provided us with a way to outwit and outplay our enemy. Like a coach, the apostle Paul gives us insight into God's strategy (the redemptive sacrifice of Jesus) as well as our goal when he writes concerning his teaching of Jesus Christ, "We proclaim Him, admonishing every person and teaching every person with all wisdom, so that we may present every person complete in Christ. For this purpose I also labor, striving according to His power which works mightily within me" (Colossians 1:28-29).

Our goal is spiritual completion, whether our own or our brothers and sisters in Christ. Our mature wholeness in Christ serves as the final score when we stand before Him one day. And since spiritual completion is our goal, it is critical to fully understand what it means to be presented as "complete"; otherwise we won't really know what we are pursuing.

How Old You Really Are

The word *complete* means "mature." It refers to being spiritually grown up. It also means to be whole, reflecting the character and qualities of Jesus. You are whole when you have fulfilled and finished all that you were created to be, both internally and externally. Ephesians 2:10 tells us that we have been put on earth to live out the purposes God has for us: "For we are His workmanship, created in Christ Jesus for good works, which God prepared beforehand so that we would walk in them."

There will be similarities among Christians when it comes to advancing in spiritual wholeness and completing God's purpose in our lives, but there will also be differences. While we may reflect the character of Jesus in similar ways, living out our individual, divine destinies will look different for each of us.

After all, your purpose has been uniquely chosen for you. It is not the same purpose as your neighbor or your friend. Your divine purpose is *your* divine purpose, for which *you* have been equipped. Like an athlete in an individual competition at the Olympic games, you have your own good works to complete. I have my own good works as well.

One of the issues that often comes up in our day and age of access to so much information is the detrimental issue of comparison. You may look at the online profile of someone else who seems to be doing so much more than you when it comes to living out their faith. This might cause you to lose heart and pull back from focusing on your own goals. But that someone else who you are comparing yourself to didn't have the past you experienced. He or she didn't face the hurdles you've faced.

God isn't going to measure whether you lived out someone else's purpose on earth. He didn't *prepare* you to live out someone else's purpose. God is going to look at you and see whether you have completed what He has given you to complete.

We all know that not every person's chronological age equals his or her maturity level. Many of us know grown adults who are still infantile in how they function in their emotional or spiritual lives. To stand before the Lord as complete, or mature, means that you have matured spiritually so that you reflect the kingdom values of Christ. It means you have become a spiritual adult and have not remained a spiritual toddler. A baby does not stay the same weight she was at birth, and you and I are not to stay at the same spiritual level that we were when we got saved. Maturity is the process of going deeper spiritually and becoming more like Christ in our character, conduct, attitudes, and actions.

Maturing spiritually doesn't happen just because a person accepts Christ as their Savior. In fact, maturing spiritually is often the rarity. On several occasions, Paul had to scold members of the various gatherings he was associated with for their lack of growth. In 1 Corinthians 2 and 3, Paul talks about the fact that there were saved people in Corinth who were acting carnal. After five years of living as Christians, they remained in a state of spiritual infancy. Paul wrote words of frustration and grief because the five-year process, which should have led to their maturity, had produced little to nothing at all.

Believers have gone much longer than five years without maturing.

The writer of Hebrews addresses some believers who had been saved for more than thirty years and yet still had not grown:

> Concerning him we have much to say, and it is difficult to explain, since you have become poor listeners. For though by this time you ought to be teachers, you have need again for someone to teach you the elementary principles of the actual words of God, and you have come to need milk and not solid food. For everyone who partakes only of milk is unacquainted with the word of righteousness, for he is an infant. But solid food is for the mature, who because of practice have their senses trained to distinguish between good and evil.
>
> HEBREWS 5:11-14

These were "milk" Christians who ought to have been "meat" Christians by this time. Milk Christians are believers who have not developed the habit of going to the Word to answer the issues of life. They are not accustomed to addressing life's realities from God's perspective. Rather, milk Christians find immediate direction from their own emotions, friends, family, culture, social media, or anything else feeding them quickly, easily, and readily.

Milk Christians didn't just exist back in Paul's day. They exist just as prevalently in our day as well. Milk Christians can hear fifty-two sermons a year, read a dozen devotionals, participate in virtual Bible studies, small groups—you name it—and yet never experience victory in their lives through personal growth and empowerment. A milk Christian is a defeated Christian who names the name of Jesus Christ yet strips it of all its strength, and since this is the case, they are unable to teach others.

On the other hand, meat Christians have discovered the skill of spiritual discernment. They know how to make right decisions based on the revealed will of God as outlined through His principles and precepts in

His Word. Their ability to see the world as it truly is gives them the freedom to avoid being caught up in how things may only appear to be.

Far too many people have been hoodwinked because they've made choices based on how things appeared rather than how they truly were. Without a fine-tuned level of spiritual discernment, a person's choices are going to reflect their spiritual infancy and subsequent carnality every single time.

If you were to place a baby on the floor along with a shiny marble and a tiny diamond, the baby would gravitate to the shiny marble every time. The shiny marble is larger and appears more vibrant than the diamond. But if you were to ask an adult to choose which one he or she would like to pick up and keep, the adult would go for the diamond. This is because the adult possesses a level of discernment, which informs the two objects' value beyond what is merely seen.

Many of us have gravitated to shiny relationships, circumstances, careers, and opportunities, only to discover that when the shine wears off there isn't a whole lot left. Living your life with a kingdom focus gives you the ability to discern *value* by something more than outward appearances or your own emotions. It gives you the skills you need to choose wisely, setting yourself up for the completion of the purposes God has for you.

When you go to a 3D movie, you receive special glasses to watch the film. You are free to watch it without the glasses, of course, but the image will be fuzzy. Not only will you miss out on the 3D elements, but you will also miss out on the regular visuals because without the glasses the picture isn't clear. Immature milk believers are like 3D moviegoers who aren't wearing the 3D glasses. They can watch the movie, sure. But they won't be able to see all that is there to be seen.

Our pursuit as Christians, according to Paul, is to prepare ourselves to see with God's divine eyesight. We are to learn how to apply spiritual wisdom to earthly matters. When we do that, we will be making decisions and living our lives in alignment with God and His viewpoint. When we live with His perspective and His kingdom clarity, we will make choices bearing eternity in mind. We will discern circumstances on earth while being mindful of heaven. When we face challenges, we will take into consideration our position in Christ.

This kind of eternal perspective influences our choices, passions, interests, and pursuits. Just like the football player who wakes himself up before the sun rises in order to hit the gym—knowing his investment now will pay dividends later—living with a kingdom focus impacts more than what we do on Sunday.

It impacts what we do every minute of every day.

Pressing On toward the Goal

In the apostle Paul's letter to the church at Philippi, we come across a picture of how a focus on kingdom clarity will manifest itself in a believer's life:

Not that I have already obtained it or have already become perfect, but I press on so that I may lay hold of that for which also I was laid hold of by Christ Jesus. Brethren, I do not regard myself as having laid hold of it yet; but one thing I do: forgetting what lies behind and reaching forward to what lies ahead, I press on toward the goal for the prize of the upward call of God in Christ Jesus.

PHILIPPIANS 3:12-14

In these statements to the church, Paul reminds readers of his own shortcomings. In the spirit of authenticity, he doesn't applaud his own gains or point to his own successes. Rather, he shares freely about his own lack. This spirit of humility and surrender punctuates Paul's writings throughout the New Testament, making him a great model of kingdom focus and one we will draw from throughout this book.

After all, here is the most spiritual, Spirit-filled, accomplished Christian man in the entire New Testament biblical culture, and he makes a point of stating that he has not yet arrived. He still has further to go, having not reached the point of spiritual maturity or of accomplishing the divine purpose for which he was created.

Paul's honesty ought to be our own. Living with kingdom clarity doesn't mean having it all together or being a super-spiritual, highfalutin saint. Living with kingdom clarity means recognizing your own inadequacies and resultant dependence upon God's power to perfect in you what you cannot perfect in yourself.

The Christian life is a life of perpetual pursuit toward growth. When I counsel people who are struggling in various areas of their lives, there are moments when they feel disappointed or stuck. They haven't yet reached the point of freedom, wholeness, or maturity they desire—despite intentions toward that aim. My question to them is always the same. I ask, "Are you further along today than you were yesterday? For that matter, are you more whole today than you were a few months ago or a year ago?" If the answer is yes, then I assure them they are on the right path. None of us would have a bodybuilder's physique after just one workout; neither does spiritual maturity come about simply through the passage of time without some effort on our part. Growth and development are a process, and the more we patiently and consistently cooperate with that process, the more our spiritual growth will occur.

Our ultimate perfection will not take place until the transfer to eternal glory and our eternal form has occurred. Thus, between now and then we are each to remain in a constant state of pursuit:

Pursuit of the person of Jesus Christ.
Pursuit of maturity in Him.
Pursuit of fulfilling the purposes God has for us on earth.
Pursuit of intimacy with God.

Pursuit of overcoming challenges and temptations.

Pursuit of glorifying God in all we say and do.

Pursuit of knowing God and allowing ourselves to be authentically
known in return.

Like a soldier sent out on a tour of duty, your life involves a pursuit of goals, agendas, and assignments until that tour has ended. And
even though Paul had the privilege of writing thirteen books of the New
Testament, even though God had revealed mysteries to him not given to
anyone else, and even though he was considered the leader of leaders in
his day, Paul knew his focus had to remain on the pursuit. It was never
to rest on his accomplishments. Nor was his focus to get hung up on the
past. The glory of bygone days wasn't to consume him. Rather, Paul was
to press on and pursue what was yet to come. And he never considered
himself to be done until he had "finished the course" and was ready to go
home (2 Timothy 4:6-8).

It's critical to understand that while salvation is free, given to us
through the atoning work of Jesus Christ, spiritual growth and maturity
are not automatic. You will never discover your divine purpose by glid-
ing through life on autopilot. You will never grow spiritually simply by
wishing on a star. You must press on, like Paul, in a determined decision
to prioritize your spiritual development so you will fully experience God's
will for your life.

God's will doesn't just happen. He doesn't force His preferred will
upon you. You won't wake up one day acting, talking, and looking like
Jesus while perfectly fulfilling your destiny. To live the satisfied, authentic
Christian life Christ died to provide for us, you must press on.

You must be about the pursuit.

Now, don't misunderstand me. I'm not saying that God will not help
you in your pursuit. He will. God will help you be responsible, but He
won't force you. The Bible is not going to levitate and open above your

lap in the morning simply because you woke up. God will not make you get on your knees to spend time in prayer with Him. He will support your decision to pursue Him, but He will not make that decision for you.

To pursue your full potential and maximize why you were placed here on earth, you must intentionally choose to prioritize your spiritual growth by pursuing the goals of God's kingdom.

Not only that, but anytime you aim to move forward, you must release the past. Paul reminds us of the importance of "forgetting what lies behind and reaching forward to what lies ahead" (Philippians 3:13). If you are going to reach the point where you can imagine a greater tomorrow, you must let yesterday go.

Many Christians are crippled by "yesterday." Yesterday contains things that you might not be so proud of—shame, pain, and regret—but it may also have things that trap you in pride, preventing you from reaching spiritual success in new areas. Yesterday holds on to those mistakes you've made, those sins you've committed, and those days you wish you could have done differently, while it also hides what you did well so that you won't try to do them anymore.

Yes, there is often some good in yesterday, but there is also some bad. And there is some ugly stuff there too. The ugly is made up of things that others did to you that you had no control over but that somehow traumatized you. It may include people who abused you, deserted you, cheated on you, or took advantage of you, leaving you with fresh emotional triggers to contend with every day. But Paul reminds us that a foundational principle in living for tomorrow includes letting go of the past. If you are going to achieve the purpose for which God created and saved you, you must leave yesterday right where it is—behind you.

When I used to travel back to visit my father in Baltimore during those last few years when he was advanced in age and living alone, I would often run into my old friends from the neighborhood where I grew up. My dad stayed in the same house where I lived as a child up until his last year of life, when he transitioned to a care facility. When I would run into these old friends and strike up conversations, we would inevitably talk about the times we used to play football.

It would only take a few minutes before the glory days of youth football would appear once again. But I'll never forget when, years ago, we were all together reminiscing about football games, and I noticed one of the men who had gathered with us was the very guy who had cut me down on a block that wound up snapping my leg, breaking my tibia and fibula. The surgeons had to slit my leg open and put a steel plate in where bones used to be. The hit was that bad. And, as you might imagine, my football playing days were over at that very moment. It's not a pleasant memory, even to this day.

When I saw this man many decades after the play, I surely didn't think he would bring up that hit, knowing how devastating it had been to me. But I was wrong. He brought it up. Years later, he still wanted to talk about how he laid me flat. He was stuck in that moment from yesterday. Of course, I didn't entertain that conversation too long. Yes, I've got a steel plate in my leg because of what happened to me, but I can't let that plate keep me from boldly walking into my tomorrow. Focusing on the past—talking about the past and reliving the past—is not going to help you reimagine a better tomorrow.

Far too many believers feel as if they simply cannot overcome yesterday. I get it. I understand. Their past is so deep and painful that it simply holds them hostage. And maybe that's you. Maybe things happened to you that have shaped you in such a way they still dominate how you approach today. But Paul reminds us through his writing that to live with a clear vision of the kingdom, you must let go of yesterday. You must press on in pursuit of what lies ahead. The good, the bad, and the ugly of yesterday is still just yesterday. You can't change it. You can't undo it. It's part of your history. But what you *can* do is stop your history from defining your present reality and influencing your tomorrow negatively. You can do this by cultivating and prioritizing your kingdom pursuit.

Are you familiar with the biblical account of the Israelites wandering in the desert and failing to enter the Promised Land? It's found in the book of Exodus. The reason why the Israelites never made it to the Promised Land in the amount of time that it should have taken for them to get there was because they kept looking back. They stayed stuck in the wilderness because they held too tightly to where they once were as slaves in Egypt. They reasoned that even as slaves they had food and water to consume. They had no risk of enemies or lack of provision like they were facing in their pursuit of the Promised Land. Yet in looking back too much, they lost sight of where God wanted to take them, so they wound up going nowhere at all.

Your enemy, the devil, would like to do the same thing with you that he did with the Israelites in the wilderness. He would like to keep you looking at where you've been rather than where you are going. Satan wants you to stare at your past. Because if he can keep Christ from becoming real to you, deep in you, and transforming you with His presence and purpose, Satan can keep you in the wilderness, going through the routine loops of life.

No runner ever won a race by looking backward. Why? When you look backward, you slow down. What God wants you to do instead is to learn from yesterday but don't live in it. Pursue your spiritual maturity through pressing on, as Paul wrote in Philippians 3:14, "toward the goal for the prize of the upward call of God in Christ Jesus."

Look at your yesterday like a rearview mirror, which you would peek into every once in a while. Live your life the way you drive. You don't drive while fixated on the rearview mirror. You drive looking through the windshield. You drive by focusing on where you are going, not by staring at where you've been. When you live in pursuit of Jesus Christ and His will for your life, you will discover the purpose you are designed to live out. You have a purpose. If you are still here, you have a purpose. God is not finished with you yet. But the longer you are chained to your yester-years, the more time you are losing in pursuing God's plan for your life.

Being chained to the past makes time tick slowly. In fact, time may feel like the slow, dulled tick of a grandfather clock to you right now. It may feel as though time is moving too slowly to get you where you dream of living. But when you learn to view time through the lens of God's eternal eyesight, you'll discover that how you use your time in this life is critical. We are to make "the most" of our days and the time God has given us "because the days are evil" (Ephesians 5:16). We are to invest our time while we have it. One day we will understand that when we view our lives here on earth against the backdrop of eternity, it is but a blip on the timeline. If we could only see how short time is on earth compared to how long eternity lasts, we'd change how we prioritize our decisions.

God knows that we are finite beings with finite minds, and it is easy for us to get stuck in a time-focused matrix of thought. That's why He has sought to give us an eternal mindset in Scripture. He wants you and me to have a proper view of eternity so that we will maximize our time spent in history. He does not want us to view ourselves as permanent citizens of earth, but rather as visitors. We are earth's guests.

After the last few years, I understand this truth more than I ever wished I would. As many of you are aware, in the span of two years, I lost eight family members. It started with the loss of my brother and then cascaded to include the loss of my niece, sister, brother-in-law, my father, and ulti-mately my dear wife. Tragedy piled upon tragedy, making the concept of temporal time, as compared to eternal destiny, much more clarified in my mind. Death will do that to you. It will clarify for you what matters most.

The years spanning the onset and continuation of the COVID-19 pandemic provided a similar clarity for many of us in the United States and around the globe. Life was disrupted and norms were cast aside, and unsurprisingly, this helped many of us identify what matters most in our lives. Crisis has a way of producing clarity of values, priorities, and goals. A great number of people made changes in their lives because of the pandemic. Some changes had to do with career paths, geographic locations, how much or how little they worked, the choice between remote work versus on-site, and so on. And some changes related to how much emphasis people placed on their relationships. Many people also sought to draw closer to God during this time of crisis.

While suffering is painful, when couched in the loving heart of God, it can produce growth. I've seen this firsthand in my own life, and I've seen it in those I know well and in those whom I've counseled. It all depends on perspective. Are you going to pursue God's kingdom goals even through the troubles and trials—which can spur growth—or are you going to sulk at the sorrows that have come upon you? The choice is yours to make. But keep in mind that the results of that choice are also yours to live out. It is my hope that this book will help you discover kingdom clarity in a way that will sharpen your spiritual pursuits.

2

CRYSTAL CLEAR

There's a story about a man who needed to get his shoe repaired. He rushed to the shoe repair shop only to arrive there at exactly five o'clock in the evening. Scanning the parking lot, he noticed that it was empty, indicating that there was no one around. Knowing he wouldn't have another opportunity to go to the shop for some time, he headed to the door to see if, by chance, it was still open. To his surprise, the shoe repairman was there.

"I didn't think anyone was here," the man said, relieved.

"You came just in time," the shoe repairman replied. "I was almost ready to go home."

Remembering the empty parking lot, the man asked, "How are you going to go home? I didn't see any cars."

"Oh, that's easy," the repairman said. "See those stairs over there?" He pointed to the corner of the shop. The man saw the stairs and nodded. "I live up there," the shoe repairman said. "I just work down here."

You and I, as brothers and sisters in Christ, live "up there" too. "Our citizenship is in heaven" (Philippians 3:20). Heaven is our home. God's kingdom is the kingdom to which we belong. We just work down here on earth. Understanding this key spiritual truth is fundamental to all we do here and essential as the foundation for why we are to live our lives with kingdom clarity and eternal pursuit.

The kingdoms of this world would have us forget where our home is and lead us to believe that where we work is also where we live. But we, as members of the body of Christ, get our instructions and directions from another realm—from another King who is heading up another kingdom. You are a kingdom citizen. Once you understand and apply that truth, living with a kingdom focus will come more naturally.

I define *kingdom citizen* as "a visible, verbal follower of Jesus Christ who consistently applies the principles of heaven to the concerns of the culture." It is difficult to be a kingdom citizen without a proper understanding of the kingdom. Unfortunately, far too few Christians have a full understanding of God's kingdom. As a result, few live with what I call kingdom clarity. *Kingdom clarity* can be defined as "the alignment of your thoughts, words, and actions based on the guiding and predominant influence of God's kingdom perspective."

If you are an American, you are most likely an American because you were born in the United States. If you are a kingdom citizen, it is because you have been born again into His kingdom (Colossians 1:13). The reason why you do not want to miss having a full comprehension of the kingdom is not only because it affects you, but it is also the key to understanding the Word of God. The unifying central theme throughout Scripture is the glory of God and the advancement of His kingdom. The conjoining thread from Genesis to Revelation—from beginning to end—focuses on one thing: God's glory through advancing God's kingdom.

When you are unaware of that theme, the Bible exists as disconnected stories, which are great for inspiration but seem to be unrelated in purpose and direction. However, Scripture exists to share God's movement in history toward the establishment and expansion of His kingdom. Understanding the Bible's purpose increases the relevancy of this several-thousand-year-old manuscript to your day-to-day living.

Throughout the Bible the kingdom of God is seen through His rule, His plan, His program. God's kingdom is all-encompassing. It covers everything in the universe. In fact, we can define the *kingdom* as "God's comprehensive rule over all creation." It is the rule of God and not the rule of man that reigns paramount.

Now, if God's kingdom is comprehensive, so is His kingdom agenda. The *kingdom agenda*, then, may be defined as "the visible manifestation of the comprehensive rule of God over every area of life."

The reason so many of us as individuals, and collectively as the church, are not having a greater impact on our culture is because we have lost sight of God's kingdom agenda. We want God to approve our plans rather than fulfill His plans. We want God to bring us glory rather than us bringing Him glory.

We want "my kingdom come," not "Thy kingdom come."

In many ways we want God, or at least His rule, sidelined.

Now, before you go and point a haughty finger, thinking that statement is about someone else—those people who removed prayer from schools, those people who have approved of transgender bathrooms and locker rooms, those people who have _____ (fill in the blank with whatever you want)—bear in mind that God (His principles, rule, kingdom priorities, and agenda) has similarly been removed from our churches as well. We have more churches now than ever. We have larger churches. But we have less of God's presence, power, and authority.

We, His body, have become too worldly to prioritize following Him as a way of life and making Him the focus of our existence. We have become too self-absorbed to make sacrifices beyond much more than a meal to a homeless man on the street, as we sip our own five-dollar coffee in our car and post on social media about our "good deed" we just did.

We have become far more fascinated with selfies than service.

We complain that prayer and Scripture have been removed from public places, but how many of our preachers today preach the Word of God? Many, if not most, offer up a seventeen-minute motivational talk, quoting from popular authors instead. A mist in the pulpit is always a fog in the pew. In other words, a lack of clarity in the clergy leads to chaos in the culture.

As a result, we have not only become a purpose-less and value-less society but also an impact-less church. Cracks exist not only in our culture but also in our congregations. We have forgotten that the church does not exist for the church. The moment the church exists for the church, it is no longer being the church.

God created the church for the benefit of the kingdom.

For *His* purposes.

He established the church to give us the keys to another realm. He didn't place us here to be popular. Like referees in a football game, we won't make decisions that everyone likes. Sometimes the crowd is going to boo us, but that's okay. We don't work for them. We serve a King from another kingdom who rules with supreme authority. And as His kingdom citizens, we have full access to this authority.

Matthew 16:19 tells us (in addressing the church), "I will give you the keys of the kingdom of heaven; and whatever you bind on earth shall have been bound in heaven, and whatever you loose on earth shall have been loosed in heaven."

What do you do with keys? You gain access (Isaiah 22:22). Have you ever been in a hurry and can't find your keys? If so, you know that means you're not going anywhere anytime soon. Or perhaps you are like me and you have many keys on your keychain, but you have forgotten what some of them unlock. Those keys are no longer of any benefit to you.

Jesus says the kingdom-minded church, which develops kingdom disciples resulting in kingdom-focused citizens, will have the keys to the kingdom of God, giving it the authority to bind and loose on earth and in heaven.

Yet why are we not experiencing this power and authority as kingdom people today? Because we are not building on a kingdom-focused foundation. We are building on the sands of "churchdom" instead. Therefore, we are trying to use our own church keys to unlock kingdom doors, and we are finding that they don't open much of anything at all.

When we as individuals, and our churches, are not kingdom-focused—when we fail to comprehend, let alone adopt, a kingdom theology, ideology, and methodology—we are unable to open heaven's doors and see heaven manifest God's will in the here and now.

Yes, we have prayer meetings, preaching, choir songs, and seminars, but we lack authority. Authority is directly tied to the kingdom. The keys of the kingdom don't belong to buildings; they belong to the King.

If we could see the kingdom as God sees it, and if we could view each other as God views us, designed to come together in a unified goal underneath His overarching kingdom agenda, then the world would have to deal with the strength of the church of Jesus Christ. But now, it seems, the world merely needs to deal with this segment over here and that segment over there, as we divide ourselves over platforms, preferences, politicians, and programs.

The enemy's oldest strategy in the book is to divide and conquer. If he can stir up division within Christ's body, he will not need to concern himself with any advancement we might make together. Rather than fighting our true enemy, Satan, our focus shifts to topics and policies that passionately divide us.

Colossians 1:13 clearly states that we are no longer underneath Satan's rule or authority. We have been transferred from the kingdom of darkness to the kingdom of light. If you are a believer in Jesus Christ, your allegiance has changed. You are no longer to follow the world's ways. But just because Satan no longer has authority doesn't mean he holds no power. Satan's power comes through deceptive tactics that are aimed at keeping us weak, confused, and divided. And any quick glance around our culture and our world will tell you that Satan's tactics work very well.

As believers in Christ, we are to be subject to Jesus Christ and His kingdom. That means we belong to another realm, our allegiance is in another order, and no matter where we reside, work, travel, or play, we are citizens of God's kingdom who are to live with kingdom clarity in our life pursuits. Clarity includes wising up to Satan's schemes.

Our citizenship is in heaven. We are merely on temporary assignment here. If we make the temporary assignment the permanent location of our focus and pursuit, we have gone rogue on God.

Citizens of Heaven

We looked at how Paul laid out our pursuit in the last chapter when we examined Philippians 3:12-14. In this chapter, we are going to look at this letter to Philippi a bit more as Paul goes on in his writings to summarize and contrast the attitude we are to have when living with a kingdom mindset. It is this attitude that serves as the framework for how we are to view our lives:

Let us therefore, as many as are perfect, have this attitude; and if in anything you have a different attitude, God will reveal that also to you; however, let us keep living by that same standard to which we have attained.

Brethren, join in following my example, and observe those who walk according to the pattern you have in us. For many walk, of whom I often told you, and now tell you even weeping, that they are enemies of the cross of Christ, whose end is destruction, whose god is their appetite, and whose glory is in their shame, who set their minds on earthly things. For our citizenship is in heaven, from which also we eagerly wait for a Savior, the Lord Jesus Christ; who will transform the body of our humble state into conformity with the body of His glory, by the exertion of the power that He has even to subject all things to Himself.

PHILIPPIANS 3:15-21

Our citizenship is in heaven. Paul states this truth clearly. And because you and I are citizens of heaven, the eternal must take precedent over the temporal. The kingdom must take precedent over the culture.

Eternity far outweighs history on myriad levels, the first being the length of time we will spend in eternity as compared to our time on earth. In eternity, we also get to experience God's presence firsthand with transformed bodies that can behold His glory. What's more, you and I will benefit from and enjoy the eternal rewards we have stored up in heaven once we get there (Matthew 6:20). We will no longer have to feel the effects of sin or be tempted into participation in sinful deeds. So much joy lies ahead for us in eternity that we would be foolish to spend more effort on our pursuit of the present than on our eternal kingdom destiny. We would be unwise to focus on filling our bank account on earth while neglecting our heavenly reward account.

I understand how living on earth in the mental matrix of this world order makes it very hard to concentrate on eternity and make choices that reflect a high value on God's kingdom. That's why it is so critical to surround yourself with like-minded people who will encourage you to pursue God's kingdom agenda and live according to His eternal perspective.

In fact, in the passage we looked at just now, Paul goes so far as to ask us to follow his example in how we choose our companions on earth. Just as a parent is concerned with the company his children are keeping, Paul urges us to make smart choices in our own relationships as well. Paul speaks of earth-bound Christians whom he calls "enemies" of the cross. These believers set their minds on earthly things—earthly desires, goals, needs, wants, and more. But to do so will stall and sometimes prevent the full expression of their divine purpose and destiny on earth. Whenever someone sets temporal matters above eternal matters, he or she loses out on both. This is because they fail to fully access God's blessing and favor in the temporal, and they neglect to store up treasures and rewards for the eternal.

It is only when we view eternity as more important than history that eternity's values are allowed to dominate our pursuits, improving the here and now while also investing in the hereafter.

Never forget: You were not redeemed for right here and right now only.

You were redeemed while being here, but for a brighter eternal tomorrow.

That's a very different mindset to live by.

You were redeemed for up *there* while living down *here* as a kingdom citizen of heaven. Thus, God expects you to bring heaven's point of view to bear on earth's decisions and pursuits because that is the location from which you are to be functioning.

Whenever I travel for ministry, such as speaking at a church or an event, I'll typically wind up staying at a hotel. When I check into my room, I never empty my suitcase and put the items I brought with me into the drawers or even in the closet. I understand that the hotel provides dresser drawers for me to use, but I also know that I am there for only a day or two. Knowing that my time in the hotel is temporary shifts my mindset toward how I view the hotel. I make choices based on the fact that I am simply passing through. I don't settle into the hotel and start hanging art on the walls as if I plan to stay there for years. No, the hotel is just a temporary facility that I will use while carrying out the purpose I have in whatever city I am visiting. It's not my home.

Far too many believers have confused this planet with their permanent home. They see the drawers and the closets that earth has opened for them to use, and they get lured into thinking that they are here for good. But God has each of us here on assignment only. Our citizenship, and essentially where we will spend the largest part of our existence, is in eternity. We are just passing through this time and space until we reach the eternal one. Don't be confused. Don't act as if you are here to stay. You are not. Your loved ones are not either. Trust me, I know this all too well.

Yes, you and I are to enjoy our time on earth. We are to cultivate relationships here and enjoy the favor of God as we pursue His will. Paul is not saying that we are to neglect our earthly lives. But he is saying that while we are enjoying our time on earth, we are to make sure we are investing our time in those things that transfer to eternity, rather than on that which, at best, is temporary. And only that which is done in God's name and for His kingdom, or according to His values and principles, will last for eternity.

This fundamental shift in your focus from history to eternity should show up in your words and actions. Until you view things from God's perspective, as His kingdom citizen on earth, specifically placed here on assignment, you will confuse your priorities and misuse your time. It is when you learn how to align your focus with His kingdom perspective that you will discover the thrill that comes in not only reimagining but also living out a brighter tomorrow.

3

CHRIST IN YOU

One of the reasons why living in America is so enticing to people around the world is that even with its flaws and weaknesses, there is the opportunity for advancement. The structure of our nation offers each of us the chance to take an idea and maximize that idea, within appropriate boundaries, for growth. This comes with being part of a capitalistically based democracy where you can use your own ingenuity to strive to achieve your best in business. In America, we live in a continually competitive environment where if someone else comes up with a better concept than yours, and positions it more strategically, you will be forced to improve yours or you will go under. This type of environment pushes businesses and individuals to have the mindset of improvement in order to remain competitive.

Because of this, one of the standards many corporations have adopted is a concept of zero tolerance. "Zero tolerance" indicates that there is little or no room for error. There was a concern years ago that Japanese-made vehicles would outsell American-made vehicles due to this concept of zero tolerance. The Japanese emphasized zero tolerance in design error, manufacturing, production, and performance, creating a shift of purchases in the consumer base. Seeing this shift as sales and profits began to drift overseas, American car manufacturers raised their standards to become more competitive in a global market.

To summarize the zero-tolerance philosophy: A company seeks to maximize business productivity by decreasing their level of tolerance for error. Now, if that is true with regard to boosting one's potential as an American, would it not equally be true when applied to maximizing a person's potential as a Christian? If sinful customers still want an excellent product, then isn't it logical that a perfect God would want a good return on His investment as well? If sinful men will get ticked off at paying for mediocrity in either a product or a service, then should we not understand how a perfect God would be less than satisfied when we settle for doing less than our best as believers?

As human beings, we will never reach a level of zero spiritual mistakes or issues from sin in our lives. But if pursuing something close to this standard becomes the goal, it will lift us higher than we would have gone otherwise on our own (Matthew 5:48). When mediocrity is the standard, people will get what they aim for. *Zero tolerance* means just that—zero tolerance. We are to aim high. We are to seek to become like Christ. After all, we accept this standard in many areas of our external expectations, yet we often question it when it comes to God's standard and His view of the time, talents, and treasures that He has given to us.

Suppose someone took a math test and answered the question of one plus one by writing down that it equals three. Would the teacher mark it right or wrong? Now, what if the student said, "But at least I was close!"? It wouldn't matter because a math teacher has zero tolerance for mistakes in math.

Or what if a basketball player took a shot, but the heel of his shoe was on the line. Even though his shot would have won the game, what would the referee say? Even though it was just a small portion of his shoe that crossed the line, the referee would have zero tolerance on that shot.

Let me bring this closer to home for those of you who don't like math or basketball. If you decided to take a flight to go on vacation or for business, and the pilot came on the overhead system and said, "Well, folks, it looks like just one fuel line is leaking but not all of them. We should be good to go." You and the rest of the passengers on board would make a straight line to the door and exit before that pilot even had a chance to taxi to the runway. I imagine you would have a zero-tolerance standard when it comes to functional fuel lines and airplanes.

We do exhibit a zero-tolerance mindset more often than we may think. I'm sure you can come up with some examples of your own, so I won't list anymore. My point is that if this is true in business, basketball, manufacturing, and flying, why do we question it when it comes to the God who made us?

Is God to expect less from you and me?

He isn't. In fact, God expects us to optimize our life on earth for eternity. He expects us to live by His kingdom standard. He expects us to plan for our futures by storing up treasures that will neither decay nor get stolen (Matthew 6:20).

Financial planners tell us not to wait until we are sixty-five years old to begin the process of preparing for retirement, but to prepare when we are younger. In fact, financial planners recommend we start as early as possible, laying aside a certain amount for savings from each paycheck so that when retirement comes, we can live as decently and responsibly as possible.

In other words, if you want to retire well, you must prepare ahead of time. Any financial planner worth his or her salt is going to talk you into living life with a future-oriented mindset. They want you to think about what's ahead in advance of your arrival there. God also wants you to live with a future-oriented focus, an eternal perspective.

He doesn't want us to just be career Christians, but rather, God wants us to be authentic followers of Jesus Christ who live with a kingdom-clarified pursuit of His purposes. I know you want that, too, which is why living in light of eternity is so important. What you do on earth will be paid forward into heaven and last there forever.

As Christians, where we place our intentions will impact whether we achieve the carrying out of our kingdom purpose. Ultimately, the central purpose we are to achieve as believers boils down to one word: *godliness*. We are to be like Christ. Consider 1 Timothy 4:8: "For bodily discipline is only of little profit, but godliness is profitable for all things, since it holds promise for the present life and also for the life to come." It is our purpose to pursue godliness because godliness is profitable, both for the life we live now and the life we will live forever in heaven.

To do this, though, we need to first understand what *godliness* is and what it is not. It is actually possible to have a false, inauthentic form of godliness. Paul warned Timothy about people who "[hold to] a form of godliness, although they have denied its power; Avoid such men as these" (2 Timothy 3:5).

It is crucial that we understand the difference between true godliness and its mere "form" if we are to be effective in our life's pursuit. The Greek word for "form" means "a shape, silhouette, or an outline." It does not refer to the full substance. When you see a person's shadow, you see only their silhouette. What this means in relation to godliness is that it's possible to look the part of a godly person without having any substance to back it up.

How do you know if you're looking at the shadow instead of the real thing? Because the Bible says that false godliness has no spiritual power attached to it. It's like putting on a Superman outfit but not being able to fly. Someone who is impersonating Superman has the form of power and of flight. He has the attire of power and of flight. But he does not possess the accompanying power to pull off what the form declares can be done. Thus, the form is useless. It's a costume. The person wearing that outfit had better not jump off any buildings.

This form of godliness without real power is called "religion." Religion gives the impression of something related to God, but it is not the reflection of the substance of a relationship with God. You can look religious.

You can use religious vocabulary. You can carry a Bible. Yet you can still be devoid of God's power. In fact, many of us know what it is like to go to church for years and not be changed; to be in the "vicinity" of God yet not have the power to conform to His image and character.

The attendance of church, in and of itself, is not sufficient for this purpose. God desires a relationship with you, not religion. When you live a godly life rightly related to Him, you will experience His power. But He does not reward religious rituals empty of spiritual substance with His Spirit's power.

Lots of people like to go to the donut shop because everything in there is sweet. Everything tastes so good. But no matter how often you go to the donut shop, you're probably not better off health-wise for being there. In fact, the more often you go, the worse off you will be because donuts do not have nutritional value.

For many people, church is God's donut shop. They want to hear a sweet song, a sweet sermon, experience everything sprinkled with sugar—without any real spiritual substance. That's having a form of godliness while denying its power. Godliness is not a service or an event that you attend. Rather, godliness is a lifestyle that consistently reflects God's character and kingdom values.

Not only is a godly person pursuing God's presence all the time, but a godly person is also always seeking to see through spiritual lenses. Why is God's presence important? Because His presence both empowers and affects behavior.

Let me share an example of the effect of living and acting with an awareness of someone's presence. If I'm driving down the highway and a police officer pulls up beside me, I'm forced to drive while being aware of his presence. His presence affects my driving. My foot lets off the accelerator and moves toward the brake. If I am going faster than the police officer but still within the speed limit, I won't pass him because I am affected by his presence. Once I know he is there, my driving habits change.

However, if he drives off and I am no longer affected by his presence, I can go back to my same old ways. The reason I can go back to my original form of driving is that I am no longer driving while mindful of his presence. The moment I see that he has left me, I can dismiss him from my mind, and my driving changes.

Too many people are not experiencing more of God because they don't live in the light of His presence. They only seek to visit His presence from time to time. Visiting God's presence does not produce godliness; it produces a form of godliness otherwise known as religion.

Mere external religion without true godliness is like having a hamburger that looks well-done on the outside but is raw on the inside. The burger looks like it's ready, but nothing is cooking inside. God's goal for you as His follower is to pursue godliness by experiencing an internal transformation that then leads to external outcomes that resemble Christ.

Paul instructed Timothy, the pastor of the church in Ephesus, to teach his people how believers are to conduct themselves as part of the household, the family, of God (1 Timothy 1:3-7). Paul also said he wanted Timothy to explain "the mystery of godliness" to him (1 Timothy 3:16). This mystery is a revealed truth that belongs to every Christian. Paul called this mystery "great," which lets us know this is not some minor, inconsequential matter.

In the Bible, a "mystery" often refers to something concealed in the Old Testament that's revealed in the New Testament. Paul says there is a mystery about godliness that was unclear in the Old Testament that now has been made clear in the New Testament (Ephesians 3:5). This is the case with many truths that are revealed only in the New Testament, because in the Old Testament we didn't get the whole picture. The Old Testament is critical and foundational to our faith, but it was incomplete in terms of God's full redemptive plan. Theologians call this "progressive revelation."

The Bible was not written as one book at one time by one person to cover all things. It was written by roughly forty different authors over approximately fifteen hundred years to tell the entire narrative since the beginning of known time. The Bible's definition of *mystery* is far different from the meaning of that word in our everyday language. We think of a mystery today as a puzzle to be put together, a riddle to be solved, or a secret to be examined at length. But a biblical mystery is none of these; instead, it is a truth that was previously hidden and not fully disclosed but that God has now revealed and explained. Jesus called the truths of His kingdom a mystery because the full understanding of the kingdom had not been made known to God's people before Jesus came and shared it.

When it comes to the mystery of how people can be made right with God and live godly lives, the Old Testament contains only the first part of that story. This mystery of godliness served as a partial revelation in the Old Testament, only to come to full light in the New when Jesus Christ came to earth as God in the flesh.

To understand this mystery, you have to recognize that a shift occurred when God moved from the Old Testament to the New Testament. If you do not understand this great shift, you won't understand the mystery.

The Shift

When God introduced His new covenant of grace in Jesus Christ, He made the old covenant, the law of Moses, obsolete (Hebrews 8:13). The Bible says that by the works of the law nobody is justified before God (Romans 3:20). The Old Testament law is the obsolete covenant. It can only tell you the problem. It cannot fix it. In fact, there were 613 laws in Old Testament days, and to break any one of them was to break them all. This means that if you are still seeking to live by the Old Testament form of godliness—that is, trying to please God by what you do and don't do based on His list and resultant sacrifices—you're living under something that has now been made obsolete because of something better that has been provided.

Many years ago, our ancestors washed their clothes on wooden wash-boards. Every time they did it, they had to roll up their sleeves and apply some elbow grease, scrubbing hard because they were trying to make something dirty become clean. Then along came washing machines. They have the same goal as the washboard, but something is different because now there is a new power at work easily making clean what was once dirty.

The old covenant was elbow grease in terms of trying to make sinners clean before God. It was people trying to clean up their messes by their own efforts. The new covenant of Jesus Christ is the washing machine, which does the same thing by a new power that is apart from our own effort. The uniqueness of Jesus Christ is the mystery of God. True godliness is no longer found in a written code like the Mosaic law. True godliness is forever linked to the person of Jesus Christ Himself.

Since godliness is linked to Jesus Christ, our assignment is to become more like Him. This is possible because God's command to us is to be holy as He is holy (1 Peter 1:15-16). We become holy through this mystery:

Of this church I was made a minister according to the stewardship from God bestowed on me for your benefit, so that I might fully carry out the preaching of the word of God, that is, the mystery which has been hidden from the past ages and generations, but has now been manifested to His saints, to whom God willed to make known what is the riches of the glory of this mystery among the Gentiles, which is Christ in you, the hope of glory.

COLOSSIANS 1:25-27

The mystery of godliness is Christ indwelling you. Paul stated this plainly: "the glory of this mystery . . . which is Christ in you, the hope of glory." Hope is something that you look forward to in the future. The glory Paul speaks of is the glory that will come about in eternity—the glory and rewards we have been talking about thus far. But the mystery lies in the reality that this future glory has already been placed within you right now in this present time through the person of Jesus Christ.

Here's what is often missing in the practical application of the gospel in so many people's lives. Yes, Jesus Christ did come to save us and provide us our eternal salvation as the sacrifice for our sins. But He also came to indwell us for the benefit of our temporal lives on earth.

If you are only satisfied that you are going to heaven one day, you will not stand before Christ as "complete" as you can be. Jesus didn't come merely to take you to heaven. He also came to bring heaven to you—the hope of glory within you. When you accepted Jesus as your Savior, He took up residence in you as the Spirit of God. He chose to enter you to make sure that the transformation you needed to take place can occur. In other words, you are not going through this growth process alone. You were saved for heaven by Jesus' substitutionary death, but you are sanctified on earth by His substitutionary life (Romans 5:10; Ephesians 2:20).

An ugly, slimy, slow caterpillar is actually a butterfly waiting to happen. But the butterfly doesn't come about by external forces or external effort. The butterfly's nature is imbedded within the caterpillar itself. That ugly, slimy, many-legged caterpillar is crawling around with a beautiful, exquisite butterfly inside it. The butterfly is simply waiting to develop so that it can have what it needs to be able to fly. If the nature of the butterfly never develops, it is not because the nature is not there. It is because the development of that nature did not occur.

When the nature of the butterfly is allowed to express its indwelling reality inside of the ugly caterpillar, that caterpillar transforms into an entirely new creation.

In the same way, every believer in Jesus Christ has a sort of butterfly inside of him or her because Jesus Christ indwells there. If you are a believer, the future glory is in you right now. But unless Jesus is free to develop His nature and character in you, causing you to become complete in Him, you will remain a crawling caterpillar even though you were created to fly. The "mystery" Paul spoke of is that Christ already resides in you now. The hope of the glory to come exists in you at this moment. You don't have to go searching for it. You don't have to study for it. You don't have to become something you are not to obtain it. If you are saved, Jesus resides in you right now. He is the source of your transformation. He is the power that will enable you to become complete in Him so that when you stand before Him on that day, He will say, "Well done, my child. Well done."

In other words, your change comes from the inside out—not from the outside in. Christ in you is your hope of glory.

Have you ever noticed just how many self-help books, life-coaching podcasts, television shows, or online articles will try to get you to adopt five things to change your life, or ten things to make you more productive, or twelve things to set you free from addiction and anxiety? All these "experts" supposedly have different steps you can take to make you a better version of yourself. But do you know what that really is? That is what I call soul-management. It's behavior modification. That's you trying to manage and manipulate a better life for yourself by following a list of dos and don'ts.

And yes, those approaches can work for a while. But they typically only work for a short time. Perhaps you know what I'm talking about. Have you ever tried a diet that promised quick results, and it delivered, but as soon as you diverted from it the weight piled back on? This is because the diet was about control and not about transformation.

In my early sixties, I was able to lose over fifty pounds. My doctor recommended that I make that a goal for health reasons. And because I love what I do and I love my family and I had a desire to stick around for both, I listened to him. But my doctor also recommended that I lose the weight slowly so that the weight loss would last. He sought to have me make a transformation in my thinking and my eating habits—something that I could live with long-term—in order to lose that much weight.

I didn't cut out sweets altogether, but I reduced the amount I would eat at a given time. And while I didn't cut out fried chicken completely, I limited the number of pieces I'd have during a meal. And though I didn't become a marathon runner, I did add consistent exercise to my weekly routine. These changes and more began to take root in my heart and mind so much so that I didn't even have to think about them as time went on. Eventually, the weight came off. What's more, it has stayed off for nearly a decade so far. The secret of the significant weight loss (and keeping it off) came about in the inner transformation, which was rooted and grounded in my love for my family and the desire to be around a long time for them, and my love for what I do in serving God and advancing His kingdom agenda on earth.

Similarly, the secret of spiritual maturity as a believer and follower of Christ *is* Christ Himself. It is Christ in you, the hope of glory. He is the source of the transformation and the motivation for the growth. He is both the reason and the provision for your spiritual completion. We read in Philippians 2:13, "for it is God who is at work in you, both to will and to work for His good pleasure." As His presence within you expands in your relationship with Him, He transforms you to a greater likeness of His character.

I'm sure you've eaten popcorn before. Popcorn pops because every kernel of popcorn is full of moisture. When you put it in the microwave, the microwave heats up the moisture in the kernels. When the moisture transforms into steam, the steam rises and presses against the shell. When the shell can't handle the pressure anymore, it pops. Popcorn pops because what is on the inside has gotten so hot that it expands its way to the outside. Similarly, what God is expecting of you as His child is for what He placed on the inside (Christ in you) to become so hot within you that it expands and presses against your flesh to such a degree that the flesh no longer controls you, but instead, the Spirit indwelling you controls you as the expansion of the living Christ takes over.

Jesus doesn't just want to be a part of your life. He wants to *be* your life. When the amalgamation of His life in you and your life in Him becomes so closely connected, His countenance, character, and conduct will not only influence your own but will also transform them. You will be like Christ, so much so that it may even surprise you! Things that used to bother you won't have that affect anymore. Things that used to worry you won't be seen in that perspective any longer. Things that used to tempt you will lose their shine and lure. Because when you intimately tap into Christ in you, His heart will beat in cadence with your own, pumping His will, thoughts, and desires into you.

Now, you need to understand that the enemy knows this, and he does not want you living from the inside out. He wants you focusing on soul-management and behavior modification with your list of "thirteen things to do," rather than focusing on your abiding relationship with Jesus Christ. If he can keep your eyes focused on the external attempts at living a godly life, he's won.

It's kind of like the trash-masher I have in my kitchen. When the trash can fills up, I push a button and a motor comes on, pushing the trash down to the bottom. All it's really doing, though, is making room for more trash. The trash-masher didn't get rid of the trash. The trash is still there. What's more, it still smells like trash. It still looks like trash. It still belongs outside in the larger trash bin just as much as it did before the compactor mashed it down. The point is to manage the trash's existence by packing it in deeper than it was before, so that I can have room for more trash!

God doesn't want you to make room for more trash. He wants to replace the trash of our sin nature with the presence and purity of His Spirit. In this we become conformed to the image of Christ.

This reality raises a valid question then: How do we activate the indwelling Christ for the purpose of transformation and not just soul-management? Thankfully, this is a question Paul answers for us in

Colossians 1:28, which we looked at briefly in an earlier chapter. But let's unpack it more here. Paul writes, "We proclaim Him, admonishing every person and teaching every person with all wisdom, so that we may present every person complete in Christ."

Paul gives us three words to answer to our spiritual growth: *preaching*, *teaching*, and *admonishing*. For starters, the proclamation of Jesus Christ has to be the central passion of your pursuit. Proclaiming Him is not something reserved just for preachers like myself or missionaries. We are all called to proclaim Jesus Christ as a part of our everyday lives.

One way of naturally proclaiming Him starts with realizing that everything revolves around Him. Jesus showed the disciples this truth on the Emmaus road when He spoke to them about Moses and the prophets. Everything in Scripture ultimately leads to Him, as does every good thing in life. Jesus Christ is to be the hub in the wheel of every spoke of your being. In recognizing this, you will be proclaiming Him in your normative conversations. To preach or proclaim simply means to declare with authority a truth that invokes a response from the hearer. It doesn't mean you have to stand behind a pulpit. Nor does it mean you have to go to seminary. It means you are to seek to motivate others toward the truth of what you speak.

Truth has become an elusive value in our contemporary culture. We are called to stand for the truth of Christ in all we say and do. When we do this, we proclaim Him to those around us whether by what we say, what we post on social media, or how we treat each other.

Now, the second item in Paul's guidance to us is a little different from proclaiming. It's teaching. Teaching has as its focus the deepening of the hearer's understanding. Teaching is more content driven, whether or not there is a call for a response. Teaching involves digging into the original languages, the context of the culture and the passage, and exploring the exegesis and exposition thoroughly. Teaching includes explaining at a greater level the truth you wish to proclaim. We may not all be gifted teachers or teach in an official capacity, but each of us can become students of the Word to learn, apply, and then share what we have learned with those around us.

The third way toward living with godliness is through admonishing. To admonish is to guide someone in their use of the information and truth given to them. It includes coming alongside someone else to help them use what they have heard preached or taught. It is the practical *application* of the truth, which includes encouragement, motivation, and correction.

What Paul is sharing here in his desire to see people be transformed through Christ is the process we more officially call discipleship. Growing spiritually is never to be done in isolation. It is only when we do life together in the context of a culture that encourages preaching, teaching, and admonition among each other that we tap into the depth of the godliness within us.

When Jesus ascended into the heavens after His resurrection, He left the disciples with a great commission: a mandate to teach others about Him. His great commission hasn't changed. It applies to us today just as much as it did to the disciples back then. It is why we have been placed here on earth: to make Jesus and His teachings known.

And as we make more of Christ known to others, we access more of Christ.

The life of Christ within you will continue to grow organically and expand as He is set loose through the intentional directing of your thoughts, emotions, and conversations toward and about Him. The more you seek to feed yourself and others His truth, the larger and more prominent is His presence within you simply because He Himself is the source of that truth.

Living with a kingdom pursuit begins through this awareness. It is an awareness directed internally to the indwelling Christ in you. He is the hope of your glory to come as well as the hope of your glory and growth right now. He came so that you might have life in heaven, yes, but also in your present experience on earth (John 10:10).

As your awareness of His presence—and your abiding in His presence—increases, your focus narrows on His comprehensive rule in your life, thus shaping and transforming you into His likeness. This continues to take place so much so that on the day you stand before Christ, you will stand before Him as a reflection of Him, fully complete in Him, ready to receive the eternal rewards He has stored up for you.

In football, the ball itself runs the entire multibillion-dollar show. Everything that happens on the field is intricately tied to the football. The players are paid millions of dollars to fight over the possession of the ball. People, by the hundreds of thousands, pile into stadiums or watch their screens to see these players fight over the football. It's all about the ball. Take the ball out of the football game and there is no game.

Likewise, take Jesus out of the mystery of godliness, and there is no godliness. Jesus is the mystery. He is the godliness within.

The prominent emphasis of the salvation experience is to make us godly men and women. *Godly* does not mean perfect, but it does mean consistent. It means that each day, week, and year we become better than the ones before.

Paul says in 1 Timothy 4 that if you want to be godly, you must discipline yourself. The Greek word for "discipline" is related to the English word *gymnasium*. You go to a gym to work out and get in shape, not to create muscles but to build the muscles you already have. The gym is designed as a place where you can develop the physical attributes you already possess.

The reality is that a lot of times we don't want to work out. But our health is more important than our feelings, so we should prioritize our health.

If you are spiritually flabby, your soul is out of shape. How do you know you're out of shape? If ungodliness is the way you roll, you are out of shape.

There's a big difference between intending to exercise and actually doing it. We wake up intending to go to the gym, but the thought of that extra fifteen minutes in bed overrules our desire to get in shape. Your workout regimen for godliness must go beyond good intentions as well. Similar to making the decision to engage in a workout program to get rid of the flab, you must make the choice to discipline yourself to get rid of unhealthy fat in your soul.

Unfortunately, most Christians are satisfied with one weekly "workout" on Sunday morning. But if you only work out spiritually once a week and then the rest of the week you do the opposite, you have wasted your once-a-week workout session. What most of us are doing is going to a spiritual workout session on Sunday and then going to the donut shop on Monday, canceling out whatever workout routine we did on Sunday, turning it into merely a religious routine. Godliness is much more than that.

You must use your "membership" in Christ to develop your godliness. It's possible to have a membership without using the benefits of that membership. When you accepted Jesus Christ, you got a membership that gave you access to His spiritual gymnasium for the purpose of exercising godliness. This workout is not to create godliness but to develop the godliness you already possess by virtue of your salvation (2 Peter 1:3). Even if you are a Christian, your soul is living in the flesh, which still produces ungodly thinking, appetites, and actions that need cleansing. The reason so many Christians stay defeated for so long is that their souls are out of shape.

Spiritual fitness needs to take priority over physical fitness. Physical exercise is profitable for a little while, but godliness is profitable for now and eternity. If you're working your body out more than you're working your soul out, you have your priorities mixed up. Your soul is begging for godliness. This is because there is great gain in godliness, and your soul knows this. Satan knows this, too, which is why he tries to do everything he can to distract you from pursuing it. Godliness is only possible when you choose to set the distractions aside and live your life underneath the comprehensive rule of God. Godliness occurs when you go all in for God and His purposes for your life.

There was a woman who had a cat that her husband hated. The woman was going on a trip, so she told her husband to take care of her cat. But she was going to be away for two weeks, and soon this cat was driving her husband nuts. He couldn't take it anymore. He took the cat down to the shipyard and put it on a boat that was getting ready to leave, and then he went back home. When his wife came back the next week, she asked, "Where's my cat?"

He answered, "The cat went away."

She said, "We have to find him!"

He said, "Certainly, dear, let's go look."

They went all around, and of course, they couldn't find the cat. The man's wife said, "You have to find my cat. I love my cat!"

Now, this man was clever, so he said, "I'll tell you what, dear. I'll put an ad in the paper, and if anybody finds this cat, I'm going to give that person five thousand dollars because I love you that much."

One of the guy's friends saw the ad and said, "Man, I just saw the ad you put in the paper for your wife's cat. Five thousand dollars for a cat?"

The man responded, "Yes, that's right."

The friend asked, "Why would you give a five-thousand-dollar reward for a cat?"

The man replied, "It's simple. When you know what I know, no amount is too large."

Well, when you know the truth about your eternal future and the great gain godliness will produce, as well as what God has in store for you when you pursue His kingdom and His will for your life, then no amount of time, attention, focus, or pursuit could be too large.

4

TIME AFTER TIME

One very important principle in life is that expectation affects behavior. If you expect to be a doctor, I assume you plan to go to medical school. If you expect to be a lawyer, I imagine you're working toward law school. If you expect to be a professional athlete, it's safe to say that you exercise regularly to get your body in its most optimal shape possible.

Now, if you were to tell me that you are going to be a doctor but do not plan on going to medical school, there would be a contradiction between your expectations and your behavior. And I would tell you that I don't think you are serious about your expectations. Because expectations affect behavior. Which is why as a follower of Jesus Christ, it is critical that you make a radical shift in your expectations about eternity sooner rather than later, which will then create a radical shift in your behavior.

Essentially, the greater your expectation is of heaven, the better life you will have on earth. Conversely, the lower your expectation is of heaven, the worse life you will have on earth. If you really want to live your life the way it ought to be lived and maximized, you must learn to live with eternity in mind. One way to overcome a spirit of perpetual defeat in everyday life is by raising your expectations of eternity.

Many believers throw all their eggs into the earth-basket while missing the eternity-basket altogether. By aiming for history, they miss out on heaven. Now, I don't mean they miss out on going to heaven when this life is over. Our salvation is not based on what we do but rather on what Jesus Christ did for us. But what those who focus on life on earth do miss out on are the rewards of heaven and the quality of eternity that will be experienced once there.

I understand this isn't a subject that is spoken about or even written about much. But it needs to be because our view of heaven and eternal rewards will directly impact our choices in history. In the New Testament, Peter shares with us how we are to develop this eternal perspective, which is a kingdom focus. He begins by disclosing a common approach Satan uses to keep us from this clarified perspective: "Know this first of all, that in the last days mockers will come with their mocking, following after their own lusts, and saying, 'Where is the promise of His coming? For ever since the fathers fell asleep, all things continue just as it was from the beginning of creation'" (2 Peter 3:3-4).

Peter begins by reminding us of the prevalent attitude in secular society of dismissing the reality of an eternity tied to Jesus Christ. The more the world can dismiss the eternal, the more they free themselves up to live in unrighteousness in the present. When God is forgotten and the thought of eternity is pushed beyond the stars and galaxies so that the truth becomes unreal to most people, then the reality of eternity no longer influences how our lives are lived. Yet the closer heaven becomes, and the more real eternal rewards are felt, the more concerned we will be about our life decisions, choices, and priorities.

What the enemy designs to do is make the world look bigger and the world to come look smaller. Those who live with this focus can easily follow their own lusts the way they want to. It's a form of deism. Deism is that philosophy of life that says, "God is out there somewhere, but He's not close to us. He has little or no involvement in the day-to-day realities of life." God becomes a cosmic Santa Claus. He's brought out for holidays, or when something goes drastically wrong, but otherwise

He's wrapped up tight and tucked away in the closet. With that viewpoint of God, it is easy to overlook both His rule and His presence. Peter went on to explain what a dismissal of God looks like in the next three verses:

> For when they maintain this, it escapes their notice that by
> the word of God the heavens existed long ago and the earth
> was formed out of water and by water, through which the
> world at that time was destroyed, being flooded with water.
> But by His word the present heavens and earth are being
> reserved for fire, kept for the day of judgment and destruction
> of ungodly people.
>
> 2 PETER 3:5-7

Peter shares how living only by what a person's five senses can validate causes a person to overlook reality and God's truth—that by His Word the heavens were formed and existed long ago. Those who live by the world's perspective—who trust in natural laws alone—have rejected the truth that God crafted this universe and the natural laws by which they swear. Creation itself shows how God intervenes in history.

Viewing the mammoth complexity of creation while denying a Creator is unreal. It takes a special kind of willful blindness to believe that you can have a watch and not have a watchmaker. How many times would you have to unravel the watch and take out all the intricate pieces, throw them up into the air, and then have them fall back down to become a watch again? To do so is mathematically impossible.

If you have a watch, you have a watchmaker.

Similarly, if you have a universe, you have a universe-Maker.

Who would believe you could have a painting without a painter? Things are sourced in a reality beyond the thing itself, yet people who follow the worldview set forth in the verses we read earlier from 2 Peter 3 willingly reject that. Why? Because they don't want any interference in their life's decisions. When you take God seriously, you will demonstrate this belief through your actions. Expectations affect behavior. But when you dismiss God, you can make choices according to the desires of your own heart and common sense. Noah had to reach beyond his own common sense to take God at His Word and build an ark in a world that had never seen rain. As a result, Noah was called a "preacher of righteousness" (2 Peter 2:5). His righteousness was rooted in the reality that when God's Word contradicted his own five senses and experiences, he chose to obey God's Word.

Many things God says will contradict what you've been taught by your parents, teachers in school, or culture and society. Not only did Noah build a boat, but he built a boat on dry land, with intricate specifications, for a period of more than a hundred years. That's a very long time to keep building something that is meant to float, especially if you've never seen a drop of rain. But that's how God works at times. There's often a long gap between what God says and what you see.

Noah looked like a fool building his boat during the day and preaching at night. His message wasn't that deep—"It's going to rain!"—and people didn't buy into it. It wasn't until the rain began to pour that people believed Noah. But by then it was too late. They had been caught in a worldview of a God who does not intervene on earth. As a result, they lost everything.

Living in light of eternity means living with a mindset that God's Word is true, even if you don't see God moving in your life right now.

Applying God's Perspective

In addition to living according to the truth of God's Word, Peter urges us to make decisions by applying God's perspective to all we do. The next two verses in his letter tell us:

But do not let this one fact escape your notice, beloved, that with the Lord one day is like a thousand years, and a thousand years like one day. The Lord is not slow about His promise, as some count slowness, but is patient toward you, not wishing for any to perish, but for all to come to repentance.

2 PETER 3:8-9

Applying God's perspective to our lives requires a dramatic change in how we view life itself and time. We live our lives linearly, from one point to the next point and so on. We move from seconds to minutes to hours to days to months and to years. That's how we measure time. That's how we understand life. Time is only meaningful to us because of this linear movement. However, God does not operate by linear time at all. In other words, He transcends time—which is why Scripture calls Him the eternal God.

We live in three phases: what was, what is, and what is to come. Yesterday, today, and tomorrow.

God lives in one phase: now.

He only exists in the present. God does not have a yesterday, and He does not have a tomorrow. He'll communicate to us in terms that reflect our divisions of time so that we can understand Him, but He does not divide time Himself in that manner. Everything is NOW.

When Moses asked God in Exodus 3:13, "Behold, I am going to the sons of Israel, and I will say to them, 'The God of your fathers has sent me to you.' Now they may say to me, 'What is His name?' What shall I say to them?"

God responded to Moses' question with a revealing answer. He told him, "'I AM WHO I AM'; and He said, 'Thus you shall say to the sons of Israel, "I AM has sent me to you"'" (Exodus 3:14).

In the original language, this statement is laid out like this: *I* (personal pronoun) *AM* (present tense), defined by *I* (personal pronoun) *AM* (present tense).

In other words, He is the personal God who forever lives in now. God only knows *now*. He doesn't have to look back at the past nor does He have to look forward to the future because both of these are contained within His eternal *now*. That's why in eternity, time will be meaningless to you. There will exist no night. No rising of the sun. No setting of the sun. Everything in eternity will be *now*.

I understand that this is hard to conceive because you and I are sealed in a time matrix and that's all we know how to comprehend. God tries to explain it to us in a way we can understand by sharing in the verse we just read that one day is as a thousand years and a thousand years is as one day. Translation: Don't use your watch to measure God's timetable because He didn't say one day *is* a thousand years, He says it's *like* it. God's viewpoint on time is outside of our scope of operation and awareness. Or as Isaiah 55:8-9 puts it, "'For My thoughts are not your thoughts, nor are your ways My ways,' declares the LORD. 'For as the heavens are higher than the earth, so are My ways higher than your ways and My thoughts than your thoughts.'"

Essentially, this passage is reminding us not to use our watch to measure God's time. God wants you and me to live from a different vantage point. Think of a person in a helicopter who has a much better visual of the traffic all around. Like that person looking down from up high, we are to tap into God's sightline rather than ours. We are not to live from the vantage point of the temporal but from the vantage point of the eternal, while simultaneously living in the shell of the temporal. We are to be driving on the highway while navigating from the information coming from the helicopter.

We are to be heavenly minded while maneuvering in history.

This emphasizes the next truth more clearly because Peter tells us that God is not slow concerning His promises. This only makes sense to us when we first adopt and apply God's viewpoint on time to our own understanding. Because when we apply our own viewpoint on time to God's movements in history, He can appear to be very slow. But that's because we are looking at our own watches and calendars; we are not considering God's perspective on time.

The Word tells us that He is not slow; therefore, we are to take God at His Word and rest in His sovereign control of time and circumstances. What's more, His delays are often linked to our holding Him up in some way, not the other way around. God may seem slow to us, but He is actually being patient with us—waiting on us to get in alignment with His will before He moves on our behalf.

This truth raises the great theological conundrum between God's sovereignty and our responsibility. This is the tension that exists between the reality of a God who is completely in control of everything and the question of what that God, who is completely in control of everything, expects from you. Because if He's in control of everything sovereignly, then why isn't everything happening like it's supposed to?

The answer to that question is that, within His sovereignty, God has crafted room for our responsibility. Just like in any sporting event, there are certain non-negotiables that exist in order to govern the game. The activity on the field is always negotiable within those sovereign boundaries. The plays that are called are negotiable within the established rules and lines of the game. Thus, the responsibility of each team or each individual athlete determines the outcome of the game, but they can't determine an outcome that conflicts with the game's rules and the boundaries of the field.

In God's infinite wisdom when He established the earth and placed us on it, He turned over the responsibility of management to us. He didn't make a world of robots who are programmed to obey everything He said. God sought to create an environment where love could be chosen, obedience could demonstrate honor, and choices could reflect alignment. In doing so, this strategy placed Him in a position of waiting on us to ultimately determine the timing and approach of what He does.

Consider the fact that it was only a few weeks' walk from Egypt to the Promised Land, but those few weeks somehow turned into forty years. It's not that God changed His plan. He planned to take the Israelites out of Egypt and set them free. It took forty years because the Israelites fought Him along the way. They left Him out of their understanding and choices, and in turn, they suffered the consequences of their rebellion.

Similarly, Abraham and Sarah had to wait twenty-five years to have a promise fulfilled of a blessing that could have been given to them much sooner. But because they introduced a fleshly solution into a spiritual scenario, they delayed the onset of their own promise. What they chose didn't change what God had said or what He had promised; it changed the timing of when it happened, as well as the resulting consequences, which are still being felt to this day between the descendants of Ishmael and Isaac in the Middle East.

Because God is waiting on us with regard to our choices and alignment under Him, we have a large say in when He will carry out the promises He's made for our lives. God is not slow concerning His promises, but you and I can slow Him down concerning the timing of the deliverance of those promises. That's why there are countless illustrations in Scripture where God tells someone to do something first before He will do what He said He will do. He desires to see obedience and faith before deliverance.

We spend so much of our time asking God to do this, that, and the other, while complaining about how we are waiting on God to shift this, reverse that, and overcome an obstacle we face. All the while God is waiting patiently for us to do what He has told us to do—as an act of faith—so that He can move forward on what He has chosen to do.

In the same way that there is a prescribed time frame in which most people will start school, attend, and eventually graduate from high school, this time frame can be delayed if someone doesn't show up, do the work, or pass the tests. God has set forth a prescribed time frame for the situations and scenarios in your life, but it is in your hands to usher them forward in a timely manner. You can delay God's deliverance and blessings by your own actions.

Living with eternity in mind is punctuated by living with the vantage point of God's view on time. He doesn't mind waiting for you to do what He's instructed you to do. A day is as a thousand years to the Lord. He's got time. It's you and I who are bound by the confines of time's effect on us, which means it is you and I who greatly need to follow God fully so that we release His hand in the history of our hearts and lives.

In addition to that, living with an awareness of eternity enables us to detach mentally from the temporal and the pull it too often has on our lives. Peter sheds insight on the longevity of this life and how that ought to impact our choices:

> The day of the Lord will come like a thief, in which the heavens will pass away with a roar and the elements will be destroyed with intense heat, and the earth and its works will be burned up.
>
> Since all these things are to be destroyed in this way, what sort of people ought you to be in holy conduct and godliness.
>
> 2 PETER 3:10-11

Since the material things that we hold so dear are going to be destroyed, we need to question why we are treating them as though they won't! That new car is going to be destroyed. That new house is going to be destroyed. Those new clothes are going to be destroyed. That money will be destroyed, and even the bank holding it is going to be destroyed. Wall Street will melt. Sports stadiums will implode. Jewels will be destroyed.

All those things that humanity clings to are going to eventually evaporate into nothing. This truth serves as a powerful reminder that we should not treat, value, seek, pursue, and grasp these things as fervently as we may do. To do so is to live our lives without a view of eternity, disregarding what will happen when eternity collides with the temporal construct of time. Even our bodies will one day be destroyed.

I want to ask you to do me a favor. I'd like to ask you to consider visiting your local junkyard. Whether it's this week or this month, will you take a moment to go to a junkyard? And if you feel that's too much to ask, would you at least search "junkyard images" online and look at what you find? Everything you see in a junkyard was at one time brand new. Everything. Those things used to look good. They used to have value. They used to have substance. But now those items are only good to be thrown away.

I understand that we live in a tangible world that requires tangible goods. You need a car to drive to work. You need a roof over your head. You need clothes to wear and money in the bank. Peter is not telling us that these things are evil in and of themselves. That's not the point. The point is, they won't last. And if they won't last, why place them so high on your priority list, even over and above what does last, which is all that is done for and in view of eternity? James spells this out for us bluntly:

> The brother of humble circumstances is to glory in his high
> position; and the rich man is to glory in his humiliation, because
> like flowering grass he will pass away. For the sun rises with a
> scorching wind and withers the grass; and its flower falls off and
> the beauty of its appearance is destroyed; so too the rich man in
> the midst of his pursuits will fade away.
>
> Blessed is a man who perseveres under trial; for once he has
> been approved, he will receive the crown of life which the Lord
> has promised to those who love Him.
>
> JAMES 1:9-12

All that we have right now will one day disintegrate. Which simply means that we ought to hold them loosely, not intimately. We ought to focus as much, if not more, on what Peter told us should be our aim—the pursuit of holiness and godliness. We are to focus on living a life pleasing to God. That must be our goal if we are to live with a view of eternity. Everything else is going to one day be taken away from us. Only that which is done for God will last.

In the next three verses in Peter's letter (2 Peter 3:12-14), he shares with us how we can go about having this kingdom mindset. Three times in these three verses Peter uses a form of the word *look*. He writes about "*looking* for and hastening the coming of the day of God" (verse 12, emphasis added). He goes on, "But according to His promise, we are *looking* for new heavens and a new earth. . . . Therefore, beloved, since you *look* for these things, be diligent to be found by Him in peace, spotless and blameless" (verses 13-14, emphasis added).

It's the word *look* that I want you to notice. By shifting what you are looking at, what you value and choose to do will be impacted. Peter is instructing us to move our gaze from looking at this life to looking toward eternity instead. It is all about our focus and what we choose to focus on.

Where you choose to look will determine how you live.

Having an eternal perspective as your priority will affect your choices and decisions; it will affect how attached you feel to the things of this world. The world's disappointments will no longer feel so crushing. Its fears will no longer feel so consuming. Earthly trinkets will no longer appear so alluring because when you consider time as defined by the God of eternity, you will have the focus to see how temporal those things truly are.

5

VANITY OF VANITIES

When my oldest daughter, Chrystal, was growing up, she loved to put puzzles together. Every year at Christmastime, Lois and I would know what to get her. Chrystal loved the challenge of taking that which was disconnected and discovering a way to mirror it to the image on the box.

On one occasion, after she had demonstrated the ability to do this quite well, we bought her a one-thousand-piece puzzle. Of course, this puzzle had a lot more pieces, and Chrystal had to put in a lot more focus to determine where each piece went. It wasn't too long into this major ordeal before she came into our room from the table where she had been working and expressed her great frustration.

"Dad, I can't do this." Chrystal sighed with a strong resignation.

"Why not?" I asked her, knowing full well that she could.

"It has too many pieces," she said, stating the obvious.

Encouraging her to focus on only one piece at a time, I nudged her back to the table. With a renewed sense of confidence and a more intentional strategy, she completed what she thought she could never do.

Sometimes life can feel like a puzzle with far too many pieces. We sit at the table—our heart heavy with frustration, loneliness, and confusion—wondering how on earth we are supposed to put all this together. Sometimes the picture doesn't even make sense. Things just don't seem to be working right. The pieces aren't connecting. They aren't intersecting. So we give up and leave the pieces lying there in a jumble.

Perhaps this sounds familiar. Maybe the picture of your life now is not what you previously imagined it would be. You had dreams that your life would go one way. You assumed you would accomplish a specific task or you would have achieved a certain status. But it's just not coming together. Maybe you thought your career would have progressed a lot further than it has. Or you imagined you would be in a relationship that would be better than what you have now. When you step back and look at the pieces of your life, maybe they just don't seem like they fit together in a way that makes sense.

If that describes you, I have good news! Living your life with a kingdom focus will enable you to connect the various aspects of your life in such a way that the entirety makes sense.

If you want to lose weight, you probably won't go to a nutritionist who is overweight. If you want to grow your hair out faster, you probably won't go to a hairless beautician. In other words, you want the person you go to for advice to be an illustration of what you are looking for in your own life. When it comes to living life, God chose a person who would be the most qualified to teach us about it. Not only did He choose the best person, He inspired this person to write an entire book in the Bible about how to live life. This book is based on the writer's own life, and it's full of illustrations. Twelve complete chapters are devoted to this one subject of where to put our focus. It's written by the man named Solomon in his book Ecclesiastes.

If anyone is qualified to tell you about life, it is Solomon. He was born with a silver spoon in his mouth, the son of a king. He was a man whose economic status rivaled the richest people of our day, so much so that he would make many of them look like paupers. He was a man who had seven hundred wives and three hundred girlfriends. When it came to life experiences and discovering how to navigate relationships, financial decisions, governance, and more, Solomon had more experience than most.

On the outside looking in, most of us would assume that he was also a man who was extremely happy. And yet the depth of his emptiness from which he writes may surprise us, instructing us at the same time. He opens his book on life's wisdom with these words:

"Vanity of vanities," says the Preacher,
"Vanity of vanities! All is vanity."
What advantage does man have in all his work
Which he does under the sun?

ECCLESIASTES 1:2-3

Essentially, Solomon tells us that he doesn't have much to talk about. The word *vanity* means "emptiness" or "worthlessness" or refers to "that which is without purpose." And so he begins by talking about his emptiness. Not exactly a page-turner formula for a writer, yet Solomon's passion for authenticity has drawn reader after reader to turn his pages again and again. After all, if anyone shouldn't have been empty, it should have been this man. He had everything that most people can only dream about, long for, and strive after. Yet his first words are "Vanity of vanities."

This reminds me of the story of a man who was dying to finish high school so that he could go to college. Then he was dying to finish college so he could start his career. Then he was dying to get married so he could start a family. Then he was dying for the kids to turn eighteen so they would leave home. Then he was dying to retire only to discover that he was just plain dying by then, never quite figuring out why he had been living all along.

Emptiness.

Purposelessness.

Vanity.

It plagues the bulk of us. Which is why we spend so much time trying to find something to light our fire and give us a sense of significance, meaning, and zest. But wouldn't you know it—when most of us discover something to inspire us, it loses its sparkle, and we find ourselves right back where we started. It's like scoring a touchdown in life. Crossing the goal line makes you feel great, powerful, with a sense of accomplishment. But as soon as it happens, someone blows a whistle and calls the play back for a holding penalty up the field. So the pursuit continues, and continues, and continues.

Or it can be compared to the fireworks during a Fourth of July celebration that explode in the air, exciting the viewers. But after only a moment, things get dark again, and the viewers are left standing there, looking for more. When is the next view of shining lights? What is the next thing to make us say, "Wow!"? We long for something to give us a sense of substance and worth. Something that will make us feel connected to value and meaning.

For so many people, life is like poking your finger into a glass of water and then lifting it up and watching the hole you made quickly disappear. Because as soon as your finger is removed, so is your impact. This makes you scratch your head and wonder, *Why am I here at all?*

Living life without a kingdom intention leads to these questions and more. Even the king himself, Solomon, had them. Life was never made to give us fulfillment in and of itself. But we look for it, nonetheless. We get lured into searching for it by our own flesh. as well as through the enemy's strategies and methodologies to prod us in that direction. And when we don't seem to find fulfillment, we aim to fake it. We pretend. Like the man who has a "Beware of Dogs" sign on the fence of his yard even though he has no dogs at all, many people try to create an image of their lives, alluding to things that they don't authentically have. They try to give an impression of being somebody or having significance. Maybe it's in the way they dress, what they drive, whose names they drop, or what they do.

People will look to anything to give them a sense of meaning and usefulness. Because if we were truly honest with each other, we'd admit that a sense of emptiness engulfs each of us in this life, no matter how high up the ladder we've climbed, how many people like our posts or our tweets, or what we own, wear, or drive. Which is why Solomon's wisdom for us is so critical when it comes to making sense of this life. Solomon's primary point comes down to one thing: When life is disconnected from God and eternity, it is meaningless.

To put it another way: *Life is meaningless when it is not lived with a focus on God and His kingdom.*

It just is.

Desiring More

Throughout the twelve chapters of Ecclesiastes, Solomon takes us on a tour of his life to make this point ring clear for us. He gives us a sampling of how he tried to fill the hole that he was feeling deep down in his soul. He gives us example after example of ways he sought to meet the deep need within him by connecting to this world in some form or fashion:

> I said to myself, "Come now, I will test you with pleasure. So enjoy yourself."
>
> ECCLESIASTES 2:1

> I explored with my mind how to stimulate my body with wine while my mind was guiding me wisely, and how to take hold of folly, until I could see what good there is for the sons of men to do under heaven the few years of their lives.
>
> ECCLESIASTES 2:3

> I enlarged my works: I built houses for myself, I planted vineyards for myself; I made gardens and parks for myself and I

planted in them all kinds of fruit trees; I made ponds of water for myself from which to irrigate a forest of growing trees.

ECCLESIASTES 2:4-6

Also, I collected for myself silver and gold and the treasure of kings and provinces. I provided for myself male and female singers and the pleasures of men—many concubines.

ECCLESIASTES 2:8

All that my eyes desired I did not refuse them. I did not withhold my heart from any pleasure.

ECCLESIASTES 2:10

Solomon spared no expense in acquiring the things that are typically considered to bring about meaning and pleasure in life. He bought houses, friends, clothes, food, fantasies, and fancy surroundings. He engaged in licentious behavior, entertainment, and folly. But when all was said and done, there was more said than done. He plainly saw his life for what it was: empty chatter, empty pleasures, and empty pursuits. He says, "Thus I considered all my activities which my hands had done and the labor which I had exerted, and behold all was vanity and striving after wind and there was no profit under the sun" (Ecclesiastes 2:11).

Behold, all was vanity. Solomon returns to this word, which he uses nearly forty times throughout his book on life. *Vanity.* It was all empty. Meaningless. Without purpose. A waste of his time.

He compares what he did to chasing after the wind, something that could never be accomplished. Despite running, searching, grabbing, and seeking, wind will never be caught. You can try it for yourself. Just step outside and wait for the breeze to come by. When the first breeze passes you, reach out and grab a handful of that blowing air. Then try to hold it without letting it escape you. If you do try, you'll discover that as soon as you try to grab a handful of that blowing air, it's gone.

This example is a lot like the pursuits of life. As soon as you achieve that goal, lose that weight, find that relationship, climb that ladder, or buy that thing, you discover that the significance you once attached to it during the pursuit has vanished, as all things do when they are disconnected from God and His kingdom. Pursuing worldly gain, apart from God's blessings, leaves only an empty hole.

Every two years or so, thousands of athletes come together to take part in either the Summer or Winter Olympic Games. These athletes have trained for what most in the sporting world consider to be the highest goal—that of representing their country at the games. But you might be surprised to discover that a large number of these athletes suffer from depression immediately following the games. And it's not just the ones who didn't win. Many who grabbed gold find themselves falling into an abyss of depressive thoughts and behaviors.[1]

A similar result happens after people reach major milestones such as marriage, having a child, getting a new job, or acquiring a costly item (home, car, jewelry, etc.). There comes about this realization that the thing which was sought after and idealized didn't quite bring about the anticipated outcome. A nagging emptiness remains, a longing for something more.

What this world has to offer was never made to satisfy us fully. Even wisdom itself couldn't satisfy Solomon. After acquiring material things, pleasures, people, and pomp, Solomon turned his heart toward the pursuit of wisdom, only to discover that wisdom didn't lead him to what he thought it would:

So I turned to consider wisdom, madness and folly; for what will the man do who will come after the king except what has already been done? And I saw that wisdom excels folly as light excels darkness. The wise man's eyes are in his head, but the fool walks

in darkness. And yet I know that one fate befalls them both.
Then I said to myself, "As is the fate of the fool, it will also befall
me. Why then have I been extremely wise?" So I said to myself,
"This too is vanity."

ECCLESIASTES 2:12-15

Nobody was more brilliant or wise than Solomon. But even he saw
the futility of where wisdom leads apart from God. The fool and the sage
wind up in the grave.

The reality of death interrupted his ability to enjoy the advantages he
had achieved in life. This reality caused Solomon to sink more deeply into
his sullen mindset, invoking emotions of hate: "So I hated life, for the
work which had been done under the sun was grievous to me; because
everything is futility and striving after wind" (Ecclesiastes 2:17). Solomon
even despised his labor and accomplishments because he knew that when
he died, those things would go to someone else, and who was to say
whether that person would use them wisely or misuse what he had built
(Ecclesiastes 2:18-20)?

Solomon discovered the devastating reality of climbing a ladder only
to discover it was leaning against the wrong wall. Which leads us to one of
the gems in this book that, when applied, can give us significance, meaning, and purpose. It's nestled in chapter 3 amid a barrage of comparisons
linked with time. Solomon says there is a time to laugh and a time to weep,
to give birth and to die, to be silent and to speak, and more. Here in this
descriptive narrative on the bookends of what our lives entail, Solomon
stumbles upon the importance of living with a kingdom mindset:

He has made everything appropriate in its time. He has also set
eternity in their heart, yet so that man will not find out the work
which God has done from the beginning even to the end.

I know that there is nothing better for them than to rejoice
and to do good in one's lifetime; moreover, that every man who
eats and drinks sees good in all his labor—it is the gift of God.
I know that everything God does will remain forever; there is
nothing to add to it and there is nothing to take from it, for God
has so worked that men should fear Him. That which is has been
already and that which will be has already been, for God seeks
what has passed by.

ECCLESIASTES 3:11-15

The key to living a life of meaning is found in your focus. This is
because God has set eternity in your heart. And while you may not know
it, that longing you have for "so much more" is a longing for God Himself.
That desire you have for purpose is a desire for Him. That need you feel
for significance is a God-placed need for His presence. God *is* eternity. He
is the forever-God. The eternity He set within you is Him. It is found in
your connection to Him.

He didn't make you for just the present. He didn't create you for only
this moment. God fashioned you for forever. The degree to which you
intentionally seek to connect time with eternity is the degree to which you
can change what feels like vanity into what truly is victory. But as long as
you disconnect the two, you will remain trapped in a loop that you cannot
change, nor will it be able to fulfill you.

People often confuse the reality of now. You are not in the land of the living on your way to the land of the dying. No, you are in the land of the dying
on your way to the land of the living. If you are going to find satisfaction
for your soul on this side of eternity, you will need to link what you do, say,
think, and choose with eternity. Life is a gift from God. He has given it to us
to enjoy. But when we make life an idol, we lose it altogether. Life without

God is like a needle without a thread or a pen without ink. To enjoy life and find satisfaction in it requires a kingdom focus and connection with God.

Anyone who knows me even a little knows that I love fried chicken. Whenever I go to the Atlanta airport, I always stop at a special place near the gates that sells some of the best fried chicken I've ever had. A number of years ago when I stopped to get my fried chicken, I heard my flight being called in the background. It was the last call to board my flight, but I was still in line for my chicken. I'll be honest, I struggled with what to do because I needed to catch my flight, but I also wanted to get some great fried chicken.

I didn't go to the Atlanta airport for fried chicken, of course. That was just a bonus in being there. To miss my flight in order to get fried chicken would have been foolish. Likewise, to miss out on the fullness of your eternal rewards because you want the temporal goods of this world would be just as foolish.

If you've been to Yellowstone National Park, or any park of that sort, you will inevitably come across a sign that reads, "Do not feed the bears." Because if you feed the bears junk food, it will not only negatively impact their health and cause them to seek to be closer to tourists, increasing the risk of danger, but it will also train them to want junk food. It will train their senses to desire human food—potato chips, hot dogs, cotton candy, and more. When the bears' taste buds become trained to enjoy junk food, they will no longer want to eat their natural food. Then when the tourists are not around, they will be looking for more tourists to provide them with junk food, rather than scrounging for their natural food.

God understands that we live in a world of junk food. We are given all sorts of things that taste good but provide no nutritional value. He also understands that the more we look to these things as our source— whether it is the source of our fulfillment, entertainment, sense of significance, or more—we will lose our desire for what truly satisfies, nourishes, and sustains us: Him. As a result, we will lose our strength, vitality, resourcefulness, joy, and a variety of critical elements that make life worth living.

Solomon was the wisest of men, and he had the capacity to look for meaning in every way possible. But at the end of the day, he summed up our human existence with these words: "The conclusion, when all has been heard, is: fear God and keep His commandments, because this applies to every person. For God will bring every act to judgment, everything which is hidden, whether it is good or evil" (Ecclesiastes 12:13-14).

In the end, Solomon looked ahead to Judgment Day. He knew God would hold everyone to account. So he concluded that true meaning is to be found in our reverence for God and His rule in our lives. It is when we live with this viewpoint that we will discover peace in the process of putting together the myriad pieces in this puzzle called life.

6

THE GOODNESS OF GRACE

Many of you are familiar with the stories of Brer Rabbit. In one of the popular childhood tales, the rabbit gets caught by a sly fox. The fox has been trying to catch the (also sly) rabbit for a long time, yet once he does, he still has some catching to do. This is because when the fox tells Brer Rabbit that he is going to skin him and cook him in a stew, Brer Rabbit has an answer the fox does not expect. Rather than being frightened of being skinned alive and boiled in a pot for lunch, Brer Rabbit begs and pleads with the fox not to throw him in the briar patch. Anything but the briar patch is Brer Rabbit's plea.

Even when the fox tells Brer Rabbit that he is going to tear him limb from limb, Brer Rabbit responds calmly that he can deal with that. What he cannot deal with is being thrown in the briar patch. Eventually, this conversation winds down to a decision. The fox reaches the conclusion that the very worst thing he can do to inflict pain on Brer Rabbit is to throw him into the briar patch, so that is what he determines to do.

Yet what the crafty fox does not know is that Brer Rabbit has tricked him. Brer Rabbit was born and raised in the briar patch. He grew up in the briar patch. In the fox's attempt to inflict greater suffering on Brer Rabbit, he casts him straight into a blessing.

What does this childhood tale have to do with a kingdom focus? It gives us a new perspective to have when Satan attempts to pull us off track. Satan may be telling us that he plans to skin us alive, ruin our lives, and destroy us, but when he does, remember that God can turn what was meant for evil and make it good.

The beautiful thing about being a believer in Christ is that God is clever enough to allow Satan to believe he is throwing you to your demise when he is actually throwing you straight into God's hands. God can take the needles of the briar patch—the pricks of life—and turn them into something glorious. He can take what looks worse than bad and make it beautiful.

This is because when you live with a kingdom focus, you discover the power of shifting your gaze from the challenges of life to Christ Himself. Even amid thorns, thistles, and trials, you know where to look. When you move your focus from what is seemingly defeating you to the goodness of God and His many blessings for you, you will discover the power of overcoming. An overcomer is a person who takes their position in Christ and makes it their practice in Christ. An overcomer is not someone who is trying to overcome. It is someone who recognizes that they have already overcome—they are only in the process of working the overcoming out.

Many of us grew up singing a little chorus that proclaims, "God is so good." That song contains some excellent theology, because the goodness of God is far more powerful than you may realize. When you focus on God's goodness, you will uncover the power to live the abundant life. As Scripture says, "Finally, brethren, whatever is true, whatever is honorable, whatever is right, whatever is pure, whatever is lovely, whatever is of good repute, if there is any excellence and if anything worthy of praise, dwell on these things" (Philippians 4:8).

Where you choose to direct your thoughts will determine your outcome in any situation. Focusing on the goodness of God rather than on the difficulties of life will enable you to live above the circumstances, not under them.

God's goodness can be defined as "the collective perfections of His nature and the benevolence of His acts." To put it in the words of Psalm 119:68: "You are good and do good." God is good by nature and good in what He does.

The goodness of God is the standard by which anything called good must be judged. Mark 10 makes this remarkably clear, because here we are confronted with the foundation of goodness. The rich young ruler had all the things—wealth, youth, and power—that most people fight to get. But he also knew he had a hole inside of him. Something was missing. One day he ran up to Jesus and asked this famous question: "Good Teacher, what shall I do to inherit eternal life?" Jesus' answer is instructive: "Why do you call Me good? No one is good except God alone" (Mark 10:17-18).

The young man was using the term *good* without realizing the full implications of what he was saying or the Person he was talking to. He needed a quick theology lesson, so Jesus challenged him, basically saying, "How do you know I'm good? By what standard are you using this term? You need to understand that no one is really good except God."

Jesus' point was something like this: "Either I'm not good, or I'm God." Jesus was helping the young man recognize His deity from a different angle. Aside from this man's particular need, Jesus makes the broader point that anything called "good" must find the source of its goodness in God.

The Bible declares in James 1:17, "Every good thing given and every perfect gift is from above, coming down from the Father of lights." Anything authentically good has its source in God.

According to the opening chapter of Genesis, God in His goodness not only created you and me, but He also created everything for us (Genesis 1:27-31). In other words, God didn't create the plants, animals, or fish just to have them around. He created them for the benefit of mankind. In Genesis 1:29, God told Adam that He had given mankind "every plant" and "every tree" for food.

Every day that you get up to see the sunshine and you exclaim, "What a beautiful day!" imagine God saying, "How do you think that happened? Today didn't just jump up here by itself. It's a beautiful day because I'm a good God."

Or every time you see a lovely rose, imagine God telling you, "I don't want you just talking about how pretty those roses are. If you do, you're missing the point. The point is, I know what I'm doing when I make flowers, because I am a good God."

But we need to realize that God's goodness is not equal. He is good to *all* His creatures in *some* ways, but He's good to *some* of His creatures in *all* ways.

Matthew 5:45 gives an example of how God is good to all: "He causes His sun to rise on the evil and the good, and sends rain on the righteous and the unrighteous." You don't have to be a Christian to get God's rain; He has ordained that certain aspects of His goodness will be available to all people.

On the other hand, God has provided Christians with the ability to enjoy His goodness in ways that the world can never appreciate. He's given us His revelation, His Holy Spirit to guide us, and a divine perspective on life that opens our eyes to see and enjoy His goodness.

If you are a Christian, you can participate in and benefit from the goodness of God like no unsaved person can. Romans 8:32 says, "He who did not spare His own Son, but delivered Him over for us all, how will He not also with Him freely give us all things?"

Now I realize that to talk about enjoying things makes some Christians nervous, but I want to show you some verses that may be shocking if you're not used to the idea of Christians having a good time. Paul wrote: "Everything created by God is good, and nothing is to be rejected if it is received with gratitude; for it is sanctified by means of the word of God and prayer" (1 Timothy 4:4-5).

Paul was refuting those who try to lay all kinds of restrictions and rules on God's people. But here's a revolutionary thought: It's a sin *not* to enjoy the goodness of God when He has provided it for us. It gets even better in 1 Timothy 6: "Instruct those who are rich in this present world not to be conceited or to fix their hope on the uncertainty of riches, but on God, *who richly supplies us with all things to enjoy*" (verse 17, emphasis added).

If we're receiving God's goodness with gratitude, and our focus is fixed on Him, we are free to enjoy His blessings. Where does it say sinners get to have the most fun? Many of us were raised to think that when you become a Christian, you enter into a boring existence while sinners enjoy all the good stuff. It's a demonic doctrine that says to be a Christian is to live an empty, boring, purposeless, and dull life of denial. It's false because as we've seen through Scripture, God says, "Everything that I created is good and meant to be enjoyed by those who know the truth" (author paraphrase).

Believers should be enjoying nature more than nonbelievers because we know who the Maker is. We should be enjoying relationships more than anyone. We should be enjoying a good meal more than anyone. We should be enjoying the flowers more than anyone. We should be enjoying creation more than anyone because we know the Creator.

So how should we respond to the goodness of God as revealed in the Bible and in the Person and work of Jesus Christ? For one thing, God's goodness should motivate us to worship Him. Listen to Psalm 107:1-2: "Oh give thanks to the LORD, for He is good, for His lovingkindness is everlasting. Let the redeemed of the LORD say so, whom He has redeemed from the hand of the adversary."

We should also be motivated to share the good news of God's kindness in Jesus Christ. We talk about everything else, don't we? When the big game is on, people aren't afraid to let their voices be heard when their team scores. They burst out with praise. Later, they gather together to celebrate their team's victory.

Then God tells us to talk up His goodness and His redemption, and we say, "He already knows I'm grateful." But God doesn't just want to read our minds or hearts. He wants to hear our lips praise and thank Him.

We are also to come together and celebrate God's goodness. Someone will always answer, "I don't have to go to church to be a Christian." You sure don't. Going to church doesn't make you a Christian. But if you are a *grateful* Christian, you will go there to celebrate God's goodness. You won't mind singing to His glory. You will shout it out. Why? Because He's been good to you.

Psalm 107:7 says that God also leads His people. Therefore, the psalmist's advice is, "Give thanks to the LORD" (verse 8). And in verse 9, the writer declares that God gives food to the hungry and water to the thirsty. Then he says when the anxious cry out to God in their troubles, He saves them from their distress (verses 13-14).

God wants to be praised. You've probably taught your children to say, "Thank you." Do you just teach them to say it once a week or once a year? Or do you want them to learn to say "Thank you" as a way of life, so that it's the exception when they don't express thanks? Many parents say to their children when they receive something, "I didn't hear you say, 'Thank you.' What do you say?"

God gives us a similar prompt in Scripture when we're told again and again to "give thanks to the LORD." It's as if He's saying, "What do you say? I can't hear you. I don't hear the thanksgiving." Praise is not complete until it has been expressed. The goodness of God gives us ample opportunities to be thankful: "O taste and see that the LORD is good" (Psalm 34:8).

God's Goodness

This is where it gets good, because as I said previously, the supreme expression of God's goodness was in the grace of salvation He poured out on us through Christ's death on the cross. Make sure you have a firm grasp on this truth: God's grace is possible only because of the sacrifice His Son made for us on the cross. We are spiritually alive today and not consumed in sin and its repercussions only because of what Jesus did. And we will go to heaven only because of what Jesus did.

If it were not for the sacrifice of Jesus Christ, we would have been wiped out in judgment. But Christ's death on the cross freed God to shower us with His grace, rather than pour out His holy and justly deserved wrath. The reason we worship the Lord Jesus Christ is that because of Him, God's grace was unleashed. We worship Christ because He dealt with the one thing that kept God from extending His grace to us: our sin.

Paul writes, "God is able to make all grace abound to you, so that always having all sufficiency in everything, you may have an abundance for every good deed" (2 Corinthians 9:8). There is no such thing as insufficient grace.

Most of us have suffered the embarrassment of bouncing a check because of insufficient funds. But God has no problem covering His checks. The Bible says that God's grace is so inexhaustible, so awesome in its supply, that it never runs out. Grace is designed not only to save you but to keep you. When you became a Christian, God supplied you with everything you need for spiritual life and growth. That's why Peter says we should "grow in the grace and knowledge of our Lord and Savior Jesus Christ" (2 Peter 3:18). Grace is a powerful gift that enables us to fully live out the kingdom life even, or especially, during hard times. Don't let anyone stop you from growing in your understanding of the awesome supply of God's grace.

I think when a lot of us reach eternity, God will say something like "All that you needed to experience victorious Christian living was available in My grace. But you didn't grow in grace and never came to understand My sufficiency." I don't want that to happen to me, and I don't want that to be your experience either. The goal of this study on living with a kingdom focus is to help you come to grips with the awesome grace of God in such a way that giving to Him anything He asks of you, including yourself, will be your greatest joy and privilege. And don't worry about coming up short in any area, because God says, "My grace is sufficient for you" (2 Corinthians 12:9).

Anything God asks us to give to Him, whether it's our financial resources, our service, or even our very lives and focus, is completely reasonable because everything we are and have is a gift from Him in the first place.

There are many Scripture passages that teach this truth, but I'll mention just a few that come most readily to mind. Paul wrote: "For who regards you as superior? What do you have that you did not receive? [Answer: nothing!] And if you did receive it, why do you boast as if you had not received it?" (1 Corinthians 4:7). Should this diminish the value of our gifts in God's eyes, or our own? Not at all. Paul is just saying, "When you use your gifts to benefit others or advance God's kingdom, don't get a big head about it. Don't become proud because of what God does through you."

Several thousand years before Paul, God asked the patriarch Job a very pointed question: "Who has given to Me that I should repay him? Whatever is under the whole heaven is Mine" (Job 41:11).

As the psalmist declares, "The earth is the LORD's, and all it contains, the world, and those who dwell in it" (Psalm 24:1).

And just in case someone doesn't get the picture, God makes it plain so we can clearly understand what belongs to Him:

For every beast of the forest is Mine,
The cattle on a thousand hills.
I know every bird of the mountains,
And everything that moves in the field is Mine.
If I were hungry I would not tell you,
For the world is Mine, and all it contains.

PSALM 50:10-12

God's Grace

With this reminder of God's goodness set in your mind, I believe the best way to integrate it into a kingdom focus is to know how God's all-sufficient supply of grace (and anything else we might need) enables us to follow and serve Him effectively. Let's look at a quote from Paul's sermon at Athens:

> He [God] made from one man every nation of mankind to live on
> all the face of the earth, having determined their appointed times
> and the boundaries of their habitation, that they would seek God,
> if perhaps they might grope for Him and find Him, though He is
> not far from each one of us; for in Him we live and move and exist.
> ACTS 17:26-28

Paul makes the point that we cannot know ourselves apart from God. You will never know who you are, where you came from, why you are here, or where you are going apart from God. In Him, you live. In Him, you move. In Him, you have your being. That's good news, because the Bible teaches that we are *completely* dependent on God for everything we have, including the next breath in our lungs.

Let me say it again: God is sufficient within Himself. He is responsible for everything we see—all creation—yet He is independent of His creation. He can do whatever He wants. Because we live, move, and have our being in Him, we are utterly dependent on Him. All that we are is because of all that He is.

This next statement follows logically from what we have just read about God's complete sufficiency: God's sufficiency means that we can find our completeness only in Him. This truth appears all through the Bible, but I want to take one of the most beautiful poetic passages in Scripture to make this all-important point.

David wrote Psalm 23 while reflecting on his old occupation as a shepherd. David knew God. The Psalms reflect his intimacy with God and his knowledge of God. God Himself said that David was a man after His own heart (1 Samuel 13:14). As he reflected, David realized that what he (as a shepherd) was to his sheep, God was to him.

David wrote, "The LORD is my shepherd, I shall not want" (Psalm 23:1). David says that if you let God be God, you won't lack anything.

Many of us are failing in our lives because we want to make God into a human. When sheep try to make shepherds into sheep, the sheep are going to be confused. But as long as sheep let the shepherd be the shepherd, they will have someone to lead them where they ought to go. David reminds us, "Let God be God."

Stop trying to get God to be like you. Let God be God. When you do that, He will let you be you as you ought to be.

David continues in Psalm 23: "He makes me lie down in green pastures; He leads me beside quiet waters. He restores my soul" (verses 2-3). David says that if the Lord is your Shepherd, He will meet your *spiritual* needs. He is not referring to drinking water or eating green grass here, because if you were drinking the water, it wouldn't be quiet. And if you ate the grass, the pasture wouldn't be green but bare.

No, a carpet of green grass and quiet waters is a picture of rest. David's point is that God gives you back your life. If you will let God be God even in the midst of life's pressures and pain, if you will submit who you are to who He is, He gives you back your soul. He gives you spiritual rejuvenation.

Then David writes, "He guides me in the paths of righteousness for His name's sake" (Psalm 23:3). If the Lord is your Shepherd, He will meet your *directional* needs. He will guide you in life. The Shepherd knows the right road for His sheep. If you will let God be God, He will restore your soul. Let Him be the sufficient God and stop giving Him advice and simply do what He says. He will direct you down the right road.

Verse 4 of Psalm 23 says, "Even though I walk through the valley of the shadow of death, I fear no evil, for You are with me; Your rod and Your staff, they comfort me." If the Lord is your Shepherd, He will take care of your *emotional* needs. God will meet your emotional needs so that you can say, "I will fear no evil."

When sheep get lost and they come between two mountains or two crevices, if it is the right time of day, the sun casts a shadow over the path. Not being very smart, the sheep see the shadow and think night is coming. Sheep are afraid at night. David says that when the shadows of life come over us and we think we have no hope and things are out of kilter, God stands by us with His rod and staff.

David had gotten caught in the thickets of life because of his immorality. He had committed adultery with Bathsheba and murdered her husband (2 Samuel 11–12). He was all tangled up. The shadow of death came over him, but when he dealt with his sins and returned to God, God's rod protected Him. God's staff pulled him back in, and God's grace covered him. If the Lord is your Shepherd, He can keep fear from overwhelming you.

God will also meet your *physical* needs, according to Psalm 23:5: "You prepare a table before me in the presence of my enemies; You have anointed my head with oil; my cup overflows."

Inside the belt that shepherds wore in David's time there was a little cloth and pouch. In the pouch were fodder and grains; whenever David found a lost sheep, he would spread the cloth on the ground and put the food from his little pouch on the cloth. That was the "table" for the sheep. Predators hung around, but not only could they not eat the sheep, they could not eat what the sheep was eating because of the shepherd's presence.

God is saying that what David was to his sheep, He is to His children. God is so sufficient that the running over of your cup does not depend on what the economy does. It does not depend on recession or inflation.

It does not depend on who is laying off or who is hiring. When you stay in God's will and God's way, He gives you your daily bread.

Finally, God is sufficient for your *eternal* needs. Psalm 23 concludes, "Surely goodness and lovingkindness will follow me all the days of my life, and I will dwell in the house of the LORD forever" (Psalm 23:6). God is good not only during our lifetime but throughout all eternity.

If you are down, He's what you need to lift you up. If you don't know which decision to make, He's who you need to direct your path. If you are afraid about how the world is going, He is able to give you sleep. If you are confused about how you are going to make ends meet, He's all you need to pay the bills. If you are not sure about where you are going to spend eternity, He's the key you need to get your eternal destiny straight.

Is there any issue in life that doesn't fit into one of these categories? Your needs are either spiritual, directional, emotional, physical, or eternal. God is sufficient for all of them. Everything you need can be covered by the sufficiency of God as you live under His authority, according to His will, and in concert with His Word. If you come to know Him and live in Him obediently, willingly, and voluntarily, God will demonstrate to you His sufficiency.

The only question left is this: *Is the Lord your Shepherd?* Only if you let Him be your Shepherd will you learn that He is sufficient for your needs, regardless of how big or overwhelming they may seem to be.

One of the reasons that airplanes crash is due to wind shear—an invisible, powerful force that suddenly affects an area through which a plane is flying in low for a landing. The wind forces the aircraft downward or off to the side with such powerful and unexpected pressure that the pilot is unable to recover. The problem with wind shear is that it can be difficult to detect. It seemingly comes out of nowhere. This is sort of like the difficulties and issues you face in your life. You are flying along, minding your own business, doing the best you can, when suddenly a wind shear impacts you negatively. Some unexpected burst of opposition comes upon you and forces you to crash, or as some say, have a meltdown.

For airplanes, however, humans have developed technology to address wind shear. It's called Doppler radar. This meteorological marvel has the ability to see the unseeable, read it, and let pilots know what they have to contend with. A wise pilot will pay close attention to the reading of the radar because he understands that radar can see and understand what he cannot. The pilot would be a fool to trust his instincts and ignore it. Just like you and I are fools when we trust our instincts and take our focus off the One who can see the unseeable in our own lives and help us make sense of that which is targeted at us with the intention to cause us to crash.

God wants you to keep your focus on Him and His goodness, as well as His care for you as your Shepherd, rather than on the things of life that Satan throws your way. It is when you keep your focus on Him that you will know what it means to truly live as an overcomer.

Yes, it is possible to "be" an overcomer in your status without experiencing overcoming in your standing. It is possible to be an overcomer in your position without actually overcoming in your practice. It is also possible to be an overcomer in your doctrine without living as an overcomer in your devotion. *The truth remains as a theory to you unless you put it into practice.* In order to put a kingdom focus into practice, you have to understand that there are unseen forces that want to keep you from having a safe landing. These forces want to cause you to look at them instead of at the One who is over them and able to deliver you from them.

Keep your eyes on the goodness of God and your focus on His guiding hand, and you will know how to avoid the pitfalls and dangers this life has a way of throwing at you.

7

A CUSTOMIZED GPS

Some people still use a satellite service to get their television programming. The way it works is that there is a network of satellites twenty-two thousand miles (and then some) above the earth. Television stations send their programming to the satellite provider, which has an uplink to the satellites in space. The provider sends a signal through the satellite to each subscriber in order to transfer all those colorful images and sounds.

Rarely do we think about any of the complexities involved in providing our programming when we sit down to watch a game, show, or movie. We just pay the fee, push a button, and expect the images to be there. When they aren't—when there is a storm or some issue with the provider—we often become frustrated and annoyed, as if satellites floating in space shouldn't ever run across technical problems.

We've come to expect this major technological advance in the same way we expect the air we breathe. And while the images it provides are amazingly clear, we are still dependent upon the equipment to deliver them. Without the equipment in place and the communication between the various pieces of equipment, there would be nothing but static on the line.

You may not have ever thought of it this way, but God has His own satellite system for you as well. It's His heavenly broadcast network. It's a network uniquely designed to allow you to operate with the precision of a heavenly perspective so that you might obtain a better, clearer life. Through His system, you are able to tune in to heaven and discover how to navigate your life on earth. Having a view of eternity will better guide you throughout time. This heavenly broadcast signal is uniquely designed to steer your life according to the will of God so you can accomplish the purposes He has for you.

When the apostle Paul wrote his letter to the church at Corinth, he told them about this satellite feed that is available to all believers through the atonement of Jesus Christ. He didn't refer to it as a satellite feed, of course, but the principles on how it functions are similar. And if you have accepted Jesus Christ as your personal Savior, then you have been granted the capacity to receive the signal. By virtue of being a Christian, you own the receiver. There's no fee to pay. It's been paid in full already.

Some satellite companies today will install a disc on the exterior of the home, which pulls down the signal from the satellite. The satellite exists regardless of whether the disc is installed on the home. But the ability to tap into the satellite feed comes through the installed receiver. Similarly, when you accepted Jesus Christ as your personal Savior, God installed a receiver in your soul. First John 2:20 and 2:27 call this receiver an "anointing." It is the presence of the Holy Spirit deposited in the soul of the believer, quickening their human spirit to pick up heaven's tuning. It is designed for you to be able to draw down from the satellite of God Himself into the life you are living so that the screen of your vision, thoughts, and mindset will broadcast in high definition. Paul's first letter to the church in Corinth gives us insight into what this satellite will show you:

> But just as it is written,

> "Things which eye has not seen and ear has not heard, and which have not entered the heart of man, all that God has prepared for those who love Him."

For to us God revealed them through the Spirit; for the Spirit searches all things, even the depths of God. For who among men knows the thoughts of a man except the spirit of the man which is in him? Even so the thoughts of God no one knows except the Spirit of God.

1 CORINTHIANS 2:9-11

Oftentimes these verses are quoted as a reference to heaven itself, but that's not what the context intends. This is a reference to earth from heaven, because Paul writes, "For to us God revealed them . . ." Thus, God has an uplink to the receiver in your soul to give you a picture of your life that will show up on the screen of your mind. This picture is to guide and direct you as to how you should live.

And just as you are familiar with going to the search bar on your computer or phone and typing in a topic to research, Scripture tells us that the Holy Spirit searches all things as our source for whatever we need to know from God. The Holy Spirit search engine allows you access on any subject matter you are pursuing when you tap into your communication connection with Him. In fact, the Spirit even knows the "thoughts" and the "depths" of God. He can do a deep dive into all that you desire to know about God and share it with you in a way that you are able to understand.

Another interesting thing about this search engine is that it is from God, who knows everything about everything. The Google search engine has to be constantly updated and new algorithms introduced. But God never has to be updated because all data has already been pre-known by God, who is the Author of it all.

The Holy Spirit's job is to give you the data you need for life, but it's your job to stay tethered to Him. As Paul goes on to tell us in 1 Corinthians 2:12, "Now we have received, not the spirit of the world, but the Spirit who is from God, so that we may know the things freely given to us by

God." Paul seeks to clarify the system into which you are tapped through this passage.

For example, if you have DIRECTV, you don't have another company's dish. Rather, you have the receiver that goes with the DIRECTV satellite feed. Or if you have another company's dish, you don't have the DIRECTV receiver on your house. You can't use one company's receiver with another company's satellite. In fact, the different companies are competing, so they make it impossible for you to access their feed with another receiver.

What Paul is explaining in the verse we just read is that there is a system of this world and there is a system from God. The receiver you were given when you became saved was from God. Problems arise in the Christian faith, though, when you seek to live your life from the old system (the fleshly nature), rather than from the new system of the Holy Spirit. Many people will go to church or listen to a sermon through the radio or the Internet, read a book, or spend some time in the Word, to tap into the receiver from God on Sunday, but then they go out into the world on Monday and tap into the world's system instead. And they wonder why they are often confused and the picture of their life is fuzzy! They lack clarity about life because they are unclear which system they are operating from—the world's or God's.

If you want the information from heaven, you can't be tuned in to the system of earth. When you are tuned in to the system of earth, the data you're getting is the world's. But if you want to tap into those things that "eye has not seen and ear has not heard, and which have not entered the heart of man" (1 Corinthians 2:9), you must be tuned in to God's heavenly broadcast network.

Christian Cruise Control

Most of us have cruise control in our cars. We press a button or two and the car takes over the speed. Barring something happening that forces us to hit the brakes, we're often satisfied to cruise. While that way of driving may be fine for a car, it's an unacceptable form of Christian living. If your spiritual life is on cruise control, it means you've taken your foot off the accelerator. I can assure you that a cruise-control Christian will never experience the level of God's reality that He has intended for them.

It's too easy to fall into this. We get the car started on Sunday when we come to church, and then as we leave the parking lot afterwards, we turn on a sort of spiritual cruise control. We just let the Christian life roll on until we go to church the following Sunday, and then we reset cruise control for another week. And then we wonder why we aren't experiencing God's powerful reality in our lives.

Indeed, you may be cruising along *right now*. My goal in our time together studying what it means to live life with kingdom clarity is to make you hit the brakes. I want to take you out of cruise control for a moment so that you start driving with purpose. I want you to understand and begin to experience how God can actively lead you in the various dimensions of your life.

We read in 1 Chronicles 14:2, "David realized that the LORD had established him as king over Israel, and that his kingdom was highly exalted, for the sake of His people Israel." David had been royally blessed. It was as though God had taken a shepherd boy and raised him from the outhouse to the White House. But during this time of blessing, David ran into a problem: "When the Philistines heard that David had been anointed king over all Israel, all the Philistines went up in search of David; and David heard of it and went out against them" (1 Chronicles 14:8).

Isn't that just how life works? As soon as you've been blessed, something seems to go wrong. We know how this goes, don't we? We're praising God for what He did in the morning, and by the afternoon we're dealing with the Philistines! The Bible says David realized God had raised him up, and then David turns around and the enemy is after him.

But David is determined that his enemies are not going to have their way. Here's where things really get interesting. First Chronicles 14:10 says, "David inquired of God, saying, 'Shall I go up against the Philistines? And will You give them into my hand?' Then the LORD said to him, 'Go up, for I will give them into your hand.'"

The enemy has come to mess things up for David in the middle of his blessing. We know that David's first reaction is to say, "I'm going up against them" (verse 8). But David has not discussed this with God. At first, David is operating in the flesh. He's decided that he can handle this problem with his human ability. But on the way, David recognizes that seeking God was not part of his decision process, and so David takes action; he doesn't just cruise along. Scripture says he "inquired of God" (verse 10). You and I would say "he prayed."

Let me explain something: God has wired the network of His people to work through prayer. Your home has been wired for electricity. There is a power company that provides your home with power. There's a company to provide the power, and there's wiring to receive it. But even though there's a power supply and wiring in your house, your lights will not come on unless you engage contact between the two—you have to flip the switch.

For your lights to work, there must be a point of contact between the power and the wires, and you are responsible for creating that point of contact. The electric company is not going to come to your house and flip on your lights. If you don't make the contact, the power that's there can never express itself. Not because it is not capable, but because the point of contact was never turned on.

God's point of contact with us is prayer. The power is up there! David has a point of contact when he inquires of the Lord. Prayer is calling forth in history what God has determined in eternity.

David starts with a question. He says to the Lord, "Shall I go up against the Philistines?" (1 Corinthians 14:10). It's a strange question because we saw in the previous verses that David is already on his way to face his enemies.

But he's now asking, "God, should I keep doing this? I *plan* to do it. I *think* I should do it. I think I can do it, but is what I'm doing what You want done? Should I go up against them?" David is basically saying, "I have *this* problem with *these* people. I'm going *this* direction. Tell me whether I should keep going because I don't want to go out there and make a fool of myself."

David does two important things: He asks a specific question, and he asks it before he takes action.

Many Christians feel frustrated in their prayer lives. The simple reason that we sometimes feel as though our prayers hit the ceiling is that they can become so general that we're not really saying anything. Another reason we may not be seeing results from our prayer life is that God doesn't get invited in on the front end. We want to bring heaven in after the fact, but it doesn't work that way.

That's why there's so much in the Bible about the word *first*. Love the Lord thy God and seek His kingdom and righteousness *first* (Matthew 6:33; 22:37) that Jesus might have *first* place (Colossians 1:18). Give God the *first* fruits (Proverbs 3:9). God does not want to be an afterthought. He wants to be God.

David inquires of the Lord because he knows that God knows more about our enemies than we do. We are finite, meaning we are limited. God is infinite. Infinite means He's unlimited. We know what is, and we can look back to what was. God knows what was, what is, what will be, and what could have been.

God is the only One who can answer the question *What if?* David inquired of God because he believed God had more information than he did. God answered him and said, "Go up, for I will give them into your hand" (1 Chronicles 14:10).

David asked a question, and not only did God answer it, He told

David what the result would be. When you get information like that, you can move forward with assurance. You are not guessing.

We see in the New Testament that Jesus Christ doesn't make a move without checking with His Father first. If the Son of God—who is God—had to check with His Father before He made a move, how much more do you and I, who are not God, need to check with God before we make a move? Jesus inquired of God first. Most Christians don't do that. We pray general prayers, but we don't invite God to move in specific moments.

Now I know what you may be thinking: David's story is in the Old Testament. In the Old Testament God talked to people. They could clearly hear God's voice.

While it's true that in the Old Testament God did sometimes verbally communicate with His people, He continues to speak to His people today through the receiver of the Holy Spirit—which you and I have been given. In the Old Testament, God the Father speaks. In the Gospels, Jesus speaks. When Jesus rose and went to heaven, He left the Holy Spirit to speak to us.

The Holy Spirit indwells every believer. He is the wiring that we talked about earlier. The Holy Spirit merges with your human spirit when you are converted. Your human spirit is housed in your soul, which in turn is housed in your body. The Holy Spirit speaks to the soul, and the soul informs the body.

This is why the Bible says you must be transformed by the renewing of your mind (Romans 12:2). Your mind is to your soul what your brain is to your body. God speaks to us by affecting our thinking, and He may use many vehicles to do that. He may have a person speak to you. He might use a song you heard on the radio. He can use a church service. God may speak from the outside, but He will always confirm it on the inside with the Holy Spirit.

But because God answers you through a voice in your soul and not from an outside scream, if you don't know how to listen to the Holy

Spirit, you will miss the message. God could be telling you, "Turn left. Go here; don't go there. Do this. Do that," but you don't hear a word because you're on cruise control. There's too much distance between you and Him. Unless you have a relationship with God—the Holy Spirit in you—you won't hear Him speaking.

When we learn to shut out the noise around us and quiet our minds, it's amazing how real God becomes in our lives. Let's return to 1 Chronicles and see what happened after David received his answer from God.

David has defeated the Philistines, and he says, "God has broken through my enemies by my hand, like the breakthrough of waters" (1 Chronicles 14:11). He says God has "broken through." The word used in that passage means something similar to our word *suddenly*. In this context, *breakthrough* means "it came out of nowhere." Out of nowhere, God showed up and turned the situation around.

Why did God come out of nowhere? Because David was specific in his request and God responded. As a result of David's victory, the Bible says the Philistines abandoned their gods (1 Chronicles 14:12). This was a spiritual issue. The Philistines came—that was the physical problem. But guess what—they were bringing their gods with them.

If you don't understand the spiritual issues that underlie the physical problems you're facing, then you won't understand what's behind the attack on you. All you will do is react to what's attacking you—to the person, the place, the thing, the situation, the scenario—but you will not react to the gods who have come with them.

So David has now inquired of God, listened to His answer, and defeated his physical and spiritual enemies. But remember how we talked about problems always popping up right when we're busy being blessed? Well, we see in verse 13 that, "The Philistines made yet another raid in the valley."

If you're on cruise control, it's easy to think that because you went to church on Sunday, nothing should go wrong all week long. You pushed the cruise-control button. But you and I both know life doesn't work like that. Not only will problems continue to arise, but they may also be the very same problems you thought you solved. That's how your enemies work. They'll keep coming back.

We see in verse 14, "David inquired again of God." This is important—David doesn't use yesterday's prayer for today's challenge. God's reply to David's second prayer highlights why this is so critical:

> You shall not go up after them; circle around behind them and
> come at them in front of the balsam trees. It shall be when you
> hear the sound of marching in the tops of the balsam trees, then
> you shall go out to battle, for God will have gone out before you
> to strike the army of the Philistines.
>
> I CHRONICLES 14:14-16

The first time God said, "Go get them." The very next day God said, "Not now." If you're not in touch with God—if you aren't listening to Him speak through the Holy Spirit—you won't know when He changes strategies. You'll think that yesterday's solution will work today.

Notice how specific God is when He answers David. He provides a very specific strategy. There's nothing vague about it. David's story shows us that God will be as specific as you are with Him.

In football, there is a standard rulebook that everyone follows. In addition to the rulebook, every team has their own playbook. The playbook is always consistent with the rulebook, but it constantly shifts because the methodology changes based on the team you're playing.

God's Word is His rulebook, and the Holy Spirit is your playbook. The Holy Spirit never goes against the Word—it always follows the rulebook—but He'll give you a unique play for your situation given who or what you're fighting against.

God has a different playbook for everybody. That's why you can't just lean on what your friends would do in your situation. God may have a different play for you than He has for your friends. It's okay to listen to your friends, but then see if the Holy Spirit confirms, in your soul, what they say. If He doesn't confirm it in your soul, it means that play is not for you.

One of the greatest tragedies today is that so many Christians are satisfied with a rulebook. They never get specific instruction. Don't be satisfied with a rulebook when you have the Holy Spirit living inside of you. The Holy Spirit wants to govern and guide your life based on the rulebook *and* playbook of God's Word.

When David came to God for guidance against the Philistines and their gods, we read that God broke through. If you are waiting for God to break through in your life, if you want to see heaven fall to earth, then you need more spiritual weight. If you gain more heavenly weight, then the Bible tells us heaven will pour down here. But that means you have to turn off cruise control and start connecting with God through prayer and His revealed Word in Scripture.

Someone once asked me, "How can you pray without ceasing?" The truth is that you can pray without ceasing because you have problems without ceasing. And as we've seen, yesterday's prayers won't give you the answer to today's problems.

The Anointing

You could say there are two groups of drivers: those with computer navigation systems and those without them. If God is the navigational system in a Christian's life, then we can think of two groups of drivers: those who are saved and those who are not saved. But I think there's actually a third group: drivers who have a navigation system but don't use it. These are the Christians who possess an internal GPS they received when they became saved, but they aren't taking advantage of it.

God has given every believer a personalized navigational system to guide us in our lives. This system has a specific name: the anointing. The anointing is a supernatural guidance system placed within us to help steer us in the direction God has planned for us. We're going to dive into 1 John 2, and by the time we've finished with this chapter you will know how to utilize the internal guidance system that every Christian possesses.

Let's begin with 1 John 2:20: "You have an anointing from the Holy One, and you all know." Right away we're told that whatever this anointing is, everybody who is a Christian has one. John continues, "As for you, the anointing which you received from Him abides in you" (verse 27). This anointing abides in believers; it's built into the vehicle.

When John speaks of the anointing, he is referencing the work of the Holy Spirit and His guidance in the life of a believer. The third member of the Trinity, the Holy Spirit, has many jobs. But one of His primary roles is to be our personal GPS, applying spiritual truth based on God's inherent Word to the realities of life. John tells us how to activate this anointing that we already have abiding in our souls:

> I have not written to you because you do not know the truth,
> but because you do know it, and because no lie is of the truth.
> Who is the liar but the one who denies that Jesus is the Christ?
> This is the antichrist, the one who denies the Father and the Son.
> Whoever denies the Son does not have the Father; the one who
> confesses the Son has the Father also.
>
> 1 JOHN 2:21-23

The switch is flipped on by the confession of the Son. The confession of the Son gives you access to the Father. The Greek word for "confess" means "to say the same thing" or "to be in full agreement with." To activate your anointing, you must be willing to be identified with Jesus Christ and to speak of Him the way the Father speaks of Him.

John says he who confesses the Son gets the Father. He who denies the Son does not get the Father (see also Matthew 10:32-33). It's the job of the Holy Spirit to give you guidance based on your willingness to be identified with the second member of the Trinity, not just your belief in God.

It's important to believe in God, but without the confession of Christ, the Holy Spirit doesn't activate your anointing. Your spiritual GPS doesn't turn on; you don't access the receiver of the heavenly broadcast network. The anointing comes when Christ is glorified, not just when God is believed in. Our whole lives are meant to be a confession, or a recognition, of Jesus Christ.

In other words, Jesus has to rule your life. He must be Lord and Savior, not just Savior. And it is the identification with Jesus Christ as Lord that turns on the switch of the Holy Spirit's activity in your life.

If you aren't listening to your navigation system you're going to piggy-back on someone else's GPS. You'll trust the advice of those who don't know where they're going, people who may not be going to the same destination God has in mind for you. And if that someone else doesn't have their own GPS working correctly, both of you are going to get lost. What's more, God's specific directions for you may not be the same today as they were yesterday. Remember, at different times, God gave David two different answers to the same problem.

First John 2:20 tells us that the anointing of the Holy One happens so that we can know. We are anointed "and you all *know*" (emphasis added). As we saw earlier in 1 Corinthians 2:12, we receive the Spirit "so that we may *know* the things freely given to us by God" (emphasis added). The Bible is clear: The Holy Spirit's job is to anoint you and activate you that you might know what God wants of you. The goal of the Holy Spirit is to make God's will, guidance, and reality experiential in your life. His job is to make God's plan real to you.

In 2 Kings 6, Elisha is preparing to face an enemy army. Elisha's servant is terrified. Elisha tries to calm his fears, but the servant is frantic. He sees an army coming for them. Elisha says, "LORD, please, open his eyes so that he may see" (2 Kings 6:17). The Bible says that God opened the servant's eyes, and the servant saw that "the mountain was full of horses and chariots of fire." It was an army of angels!

Elisha had the anointing so he could see things the servant didn't see. The anointing helps you see with spiritual sight so that you know how to react in the circumstances of life.

Abide with God

As Christians who have confessed Christ, we all have this personal GPS that's ready to show us exactly what God wants for us. The question is, *How do you get this thing working?* Consider the word John repeats again and again: *abide*. He's already told us that you activate your anointing through your identification with Christ. But then he says:

> Let what you heard from the beginning abide in you. If what you
> heard from the beginning abides in you, then you too will abide
> in the Son and in the Father.
>
> 1 JOHN 2:24, ESV

> As for you, the anointing which you received from Him abides
> in you, and you have no need for anyone to teach you; but as His
> anointing teaches you about all things, and is true and is not a
> lie, and just as it has taught you, you abide in Him. Now, little
> children, abide in Him.
>
> 1 JOHN 2:27-28

The way to press the accelerator in your spiritual life is to *abide*. The Greek word for abiding is *mino*. It means "to stay" or as we might say, "to hang out." John is telling us to hang out with the Son and the Father.

He continues in verse 27: "The anointing which you received from Him abides in you, and you have no need for anyone to teach you."

That's an interesting phrase; John says if you have the anointing you don't need anyone to teach you. Now, keep in mind that John himself is writing these words to teach others. He is teaching, but at the same time he is saying you won't need anyone to teach you. You might think that's contradictory, but what John means is once you have the anointing you no longer need the wisdom of men who reject God. If you have a GPS in your car, you don't need to call someone who doesn't have one to figure out how to get to where you're going. You already have an option that knows the contingencies.

Because so many Christians won't accept this principle, their guidance system doesn't work. They have to live without the benefit of the specific personal guidance of God's Holy Spirit.

The good news is, John has told us what we need to do to merge our rulebook with a playbook. We must abide. Stay neurally linked to God so you don't introduce fallible human wisdom that will cloud your connection. Confess Christ as a way of life. Look to the Scripture and the Holy Spirit for guidance.

I once had a problem with my lawn. The sprinkler system wasn't working so I called the company and asked for a service repairman to come to my house. When he arrived, I said, "I don't have power; the sprinkler system won't come on."

The man checked it out, and then he came to me and said, "I found your problem. Your power is fine. Your connection is not in place, and the disconnect stopped the power from getting to the sprinkler system." The problem wasn't that there wasn't sufficient power; the issue was that a connection wasn't maintained.

If, as a believer, you aren't seeing God's hand in your life, you don't have a power problem. You have an abiding problem. One of my favorite verses from John is found in John 15:7: "If you abide in Me, and My words abide in you, ask whatever you wish, and it will be done for you." This verse makes it clear that the way you get answered prayers is through a connection. The Holy Spirit is only going to do what Jesus agrees to. Jesus is only going to do what the Father agrees to. If you want something from the Father, the Son has to agree with it, the Holy Spirit has to agree with the Son, and then you have to agree with the Holy Spirit. But if you're not abiding, then you don't even know what they're agreeing about.

A question I get asked a lot as a preacher is how to discern between the Spirit's leading and the flesh, or even Satan's deception. It's an excellent question and one that we all deal with on a regular basis. After all, it was Satan who deceived Eve in the Garden and, as the master of deception, seeks to do the same with us.

There are a few key words that I go to when explaining how God's leading is made known in our lives. These words are *revelation, illumination, confirmation, application,* and *transformation.* We'll look at these one at a time, but what we're heading toward is an understanding that God's revelation is accompanied by illumination and validated by confirmation so that you can make an application. All these combine to transform you into that which Paul writes about in Romans 12:2, closer to the mind of Christ. It takes these key elements to bring about discernment of His will and guidance, as you tap into the Holy Spirit's communication within you. Let's break each element down and see what it really means.

We begin with *revelation.* Revelation is what God reveals, and it comes in two forms. First, there's general revelation, which God reveals in nature. Scientists study general revelation, even if some of them don't recognize it as such. For example, Scripture tells us that "the heavens declare the glory of God" (Psalm 19:1, ESV) and that God has made Himself known through nature (Romans 1:20). But then there is also special revelation. Special revelation is not confined to creation pointing to the Creator. We also find special revelation in the inspired Word of God. Truth has been disclosed to us through Scripture.

Every question you can ask has two answers: God's answer and everybody else's. When you have a question, you can always assume revelation from God's Word is 100 percent accurate. But what if the revelation you find in Scripture is not specific to your individual situation? This brings us to the next element.

Illumination means to make something visible. Illumination is designed for you to understand and see a manifestation of what was said. The Bible tells you what is said, and the Holy Spirit takes what was said and creates in your mind a picture, a thought, or a desire of how that revelation is to be understood and applied in your specific situation. You read and study the revelation, and the Holy Spirit illuminates that revelation so that you can see its meaning and relevancy.

The apostle Paul talks specifically about the illuminating role of the Holy Spirit. He tells us how the Spirit freely gives us the thoughts of God that we may know Him and His will more clearly (1 Corinthians 2:10-13). It's when God's revelation gets personalized inside of you that you begin to understand. God brings thoughts to your mind. He brings desires to your heart. He creates something on the inside because, remember, the anointing abides in you. God moves in you to guide you to a particular direction.

So if you start with revelation and you have your guidance system turned on, you will begin to experience illumination, or the transformation of the mind. But then the big question—the one everyone wants to know—is, "How do I know for sure that this illumination truly was from God and not just me making it up?"

It's time to look at our third word: *confirmation*. Scripture teaches that by two or three witnesses a matter is confirmed (Deuteronomy 19:15; Matthew 18:16; 2 Corinthians 13:1). Confirmation happens when God does something outside of you that connects with what He is saying inside of you. In other words, He does something completely outside of your control that validates your illumination. Once the Holy Spirit takes the revelation (what you read) and gives you a specific illumination, then it's time to look for His confirmation.

Confirmation can take a million different forms. God may use a person. He might use a situation or a song. He can use something as simple as a comment. He can use anything that will bring validation and verification of the illumination you received through revelation.

Once the Holy Spirit confirms your illumination, it's time for you to act. It's time to make an *application* of the revelation that was illuminated and for which you received confirmation. Let's look at how all this—revelation, illumination, confirmation, and application—might work in real life.

A young wife thinks she may be pregnant. So she goes to the drugstore and gets a pregnancy test kit. She reads the directions, which tell her how to use the kit. Then she uses the test, and the results tell her that she's pregnant.

The test reveals her pregnancy to her. She's had a revelation. Next, she'll go to a doctor. The nurse does a sonogram. The sonogram illuminates what's already been revealed to her.

Every parent knows that simply knowing you're pregnant is different from seeing the baby in the womb. The sonogram has been a powerful illumination of her revelation. The nurse confirms what the pregnancy test revealed and the sonogram illuminated. The nurse, who has confirmed all the signs, is someone completely separate from the young woman. Finally, the woman has the opportunity to make application and prepare to bring a child into the world.

You and I make decisions every day. But when you start using revelation to inform your applications, you can bet that you will start to experience spiritual *transformation*. You start the process by connecting with God through prayer. You listen for His answers through the Holy Spirit and maintain your connection with Him by abiding.

Once God shows you that He can talk to you, lead you, guide you, direct you, and govern you, you are never going to go back to being a cruise-control Christian. When you experience God leading your life directly and specifically, you are going to hold tight to that personal guidance system.

The best news is that if you've accepted Jesus Christ, you already have the anointing. The wiring is in place and your customized GPS is running. It's time to start abiding—to start drawing closer to Him—so that you can begin living from the vantage point of a heavenly informed perspective.

8

~

MORE THAN A FEELING

If you watch docudramas or any crime shows on television, you've probably come across one or more exposés on love gone wrong. What started as an innocent attraction and flirtation turned into a disaster of epic proportions. Some stories involve fraud, theft, and even murder. When watching shows like this, you can see how easy it could have been for the people to get out of the toxic relationship early on. Hindsight is always 20/20, and of course, the viewers have the extra bonus of not only hindsight but foresight through foreshadowing. Still, watching these seemingly loving relationships turn into situations of abuse, mind-control, manipulation, and more, is eye-opening.

While the stories that wind up in documentaries or movies are typically extreme examples, most of us can pinpoint connections in our own lives where we made choices that ultimately ushered in destruction. It could be with a person, a desire, dream, passion, pursuit, video game, hobby, conspiracy theory, and so on. When we started out, the connection seemed innocent enough. But as time progressed, that connection proved to be destructive to our emotions, focus, finances, other relationships, and more.

God speaks to us in His Word about these fatal attractions. He talks clearly concerning those connections that are costly to our spiritual lives.

In fact, so passionate is He that we avoid them, that in 1 John 2, God tells us about a love that He hates. It is a love that sits outside of His blessing and favor. It is the love of this world. This love, when it is entertained, erects a barrier between God's presence and our experience of that presence, resulting in a wealth of disaster. Rolled up within this love of the world are its own ramifications and consequences aimed at destroying our lives.

Many Christians want to know why God seems so far away. They wonder why—regardless of their religious activities and pursuits—they can't appear to get close to Him. They ask why He doesn't seem to hear their prayers. I would like to suggest that one reason for this lies in this worldly fatal attraction—this fatal love.

It is in loving the world that all hell is free to break loose in our lives. When we focus on what the world offers, we lose focus on what matters most. And by allowing ourselves to be courted by this one connection, we stall both the favor and blessings of God.

So critical is this truth that God instructs us plainly against it:

Do not love the world nor the things in the world. If anyone loves the world, the love of the Father is not in him. For all that is in the world, the lust of the flesh and the lust of the eyes and the boastful pride of life, is not from the Father, but is from the world. The world is passing away, and also its lusts; but the one who does the will of God lives forever.

I JOHN 2:15-17

It is clear from what we just read that we are not to love the world, nor the things of this world. But what are the things of this world and how do we define them? The Greek word for "world" can also be expressed as "cosmos." When we talk about the physical cosmos, we are talking about the earth. In fact, *the world* can refer to any number of things.

For example, if I talk to you about the world of finance, you know that I am including banks, credit unions, Wall Street, and the like. Or if I talk to you about the world of politics, this would include the White House, the political parties, laws, governances, and more. The world of sports involves various events, games, teams, and so on. The world of fashion consists of the fashion district, designers, runways, and many other elements. The different aspects surrounding the subject align with and plug into it.

In the context of these instructions given in 1 John, God is talking to us about the spiritual cosmos. He's not talking about a physical place, but rather a spiritual reality located on the physical place called the world.

Thus, when God speaks to us about not loving the "world," He is not talking about only one thing. He is referring to myriad things that link into the core of that one thing. He is referencing that organized, planned system designed to draw you away from His will and His kingdom rule over all.

The world can be defined as "that system headed by Satan that leaves God out." As we see in 1 John 5:19, "We know that we are of God, and that the whole world lies in the power of the evil one." The world lies under Satan's influence and dominion. The reason God doesn't want you or me to love the world is because His enemy runs it. The world is operated by Satan himself. It is Satan's goal to get you to not merely be in the world but also to fall in love with it.

And while God is not trying to get you to leave the world either—He has placed you here for a purpose—He does warn about falling in love with it. John 17:15 says, "I do not ask You to take them out of the world, but to keep them from the evil one." This verse reveals Jesus' plea that we remain in this system protected by God Himself so that we can carry out purposes of good in advancing God's kingdom on earth.

The direction not to fall in love with the world is not a calling for all of us to retreat to a monastery in some faraway land. He is not instructing us to avoid the world. Rather, God is instructing Christians to live in the world without loving its ways.

To love something is to seek its highest good and advancement as a priority over all else. It is to look to it for guidance and instruction, to seek its direction for the dictates of your heart. It is to seek to please it first, rather than yourself. To love the world is not merely related to your emotions or your affection. To love the world means that your decisions align under the world's value system above all else.

When you are faced with a decision to follow God or to follow the world, your choice will reflect which one you love most. God does not wish to be second to His archenemy, the evil one, when it comes to your decisions. The familiar verse in Matthew 6:33 states this clearly: "But seek first His kingdom and His righteousness, and all these things will be added to you." God deserves to be first in your thoughts, words, and actions. When you put Him first, He guides and directs you according to His will. He causes all things to work together for His glory—and for your good (Romans 8:28).

Romans 12:2 describes this process of growth God desires from us and its outcome when it speaks to the goal of transformation. We read, "And do not be conformed to this world, but be transformed by the renewing of your mind, so that you may prove what the will of God is, that which is good and acceptable and perfect." The word *conformed* means to be pressured by something into a similar fashion as that very thing. Think of a potter shaping clay; he uses external pressure to cause it to yield to the shape he desires. To conform to the world means to be shaped by the world and the world's values. It is to seek the good of the world's systems over and above God's will and kingdom values. In essence, to love the world means to exclude God while choosing Satan's priorities over God's. To be conformed to the world takes place when you remove the love for God within you. You cannot truly embrace the love of both the world and God simultaneously. As we saw earlier in

1 John 2:15, "If anyone loves the world, the love of the Father is not in him."

That is the cost.

To love the world is to relinquish love for the Father.

Please note that there are no exceptions here. It doesn't matter who you are. If you love the world, you don't truly love God. Now, certainly you will retain your legal relationship with God because that is predicated on the atonement of Jesus Christ, but what you will lose is your experiential loving relationship with Him.

If we only realized how much we lose by loving the world—that it is a trade and not an addition—I think there would be far fewer of us choosing to value the evil one's ways over the Lord. Loving the world keeps you from cultivating an internal atmosphere where you are fully experiencing God's manifest presence, His proximity, and His will operating in your life.

Galatians 1:3-4 explains how God views the world: "Grace to you and peace from God our Father and the Lord Jesus Christ, who gave Himself for our sins so that He might rescue us from this present evil age, according to the will of our God and Father." God did not save us to fall in love with the world. No, He saved us to deliver us from the world, even while we are still functioning within it. One of the reasons many Christians cannot and do not come into contact with the manifest presence of God and His reality in their lives is because they want to hold on to the world as well. But you can't have both.

It is like the old trap that hunters used to set for monkeys; they would place a piece of food into a glass jar. The food would tempt the monkey to reach in the jar and grab it. But the item would be large enough that when the monkey reached in and grabbed it, the size of the monkey's closed fist would now be too large to pull back out of the jar. As the monkey tried to maneuver its fist out of the jar, it would come under the conclusion that it was now stuck. The monkey would eventually give up. The thought of releasing the treasured find would not occur to the monkey. With a simple letting go of the desired treat, the monkey could escape the trap. But the monkey couldn't have the treat and its freedom at the same time. So the monkey lost its freedom in its insatiable desire for the treat.

Similarly, Satan lays out before us treat after treat after sparkly, delicious, luscious treat. He doesn't explain that when we reach for them, we will be giving up the freedom to live the abundant life that comes from the manifold presence of God's love within us. Satan simply presents the treats of this world and invites us to enjoy them. But when we shift our focus to enjoying them, we discover that these treats come with a cost too high to pay.

Friendship with the World

Loving the world is not merely a feeling. It is a decision about where you will place your focus and what you choose to grasp and hold tightly to. It's a choice to relinquish your commitment to God, and the holiness to which you are called, for a temporary, tangible hit of worldly gain.

If you truly desire to have closeness with God and answers to your prayers, and to witness the Lord coming through for you in ways you could only imagine, you must let go of the things of this world and focus your attention on God alone.

To love the world is like a bride loving the ring more than the groom who gave it. It's loving the flash and dazzle of the gift rather than the giver. And just as a groom would be hurt and distraught to discover his bride chose the ring over him, God does not take our loving of the world any less harshly: "You adulteresses, do you not know that friendship with the world is hostility toward God? Therefore whoever wishes to be a friend of the world makes himself an enemy of God" (James 4:4).

Not only do you lose out on the experience of God's reality in your life, but when you choose to love the world, you choose to join Satan in becoming God's adversary. Friendship with the world puts you in conflict with God. It leads to behavior that takes you in the opposite direction from God's destiny for your life. We see an example of this in 2 Timothy 4:10: "For Demas, having loved this present world, has deserted me and gone to Thessalonica; Crescens has gone to Galatia, Titus to Dalmatia." Paul publicly named those who once professed love for Christ and a call to kingdom building, but who had fallen away, having been enticed by a love for the world and its values.

Yet before we point fingers at others who have done this, we need to remember how easy it is to be drawn into loving the world. Anyone can fall prey to this trap, especially because our contemporary culture revolves so heavily around public acceptance and approval. We want the world to like us. But for the world to like us, we need to make ourselves likable. We want the world to accept and embrace us. But for the world to accept and embrace us, we must accept and embrace the world.

Having the world's likes on your life-posts is the opposite of what Jesus Christ said would happen if you follow Him: "If the world hates you, you know that it has hated Me before it hated you. If you were of the world, the world would love its own; but because you are not of the world, but I chose you out of the world, because of this the world hates you" (John 15:18-19). Jesus said plainly that you can't have both. You can't have the love of the world and the experiential love of God at the same time. You can't be a fan of both the teams playing against each other. You can't cheer when one moves the ball and cheer again when the other stops them from moving the ball.

Similarly, you can't listen to AM radio if you are tuned in to the FM channel. And vice versa. Yet that's what most of us try to do. We seek to love God on Sunday—or love God when we need something—only to shift back over to loving the world the rest of the time. Then we wonder why there is static on the line. There is static on the line because God and Satan do not operate on the same frequency.

Scripture outlines for us the frequency on which Satan functions. It is the same frequency we all were on prior to conversion in Jesus Christ: "And you were dead in your trespasses and sins, in which you formerly walked according to the course of this world, according to the prince of the power of the air, of the spirit that is now working in the sons of disobedience" (Ephesians 2:1-2). Satan is the prince of the power of this world's atmosphere, and alignment with him in any way is alignment with the spirit of disobedience. It is a returning to the old nature from which you were redeemed through the blood of Jesus Christ.

This reminds me of a story of a man who desired to get away from the hustle and bustle of life. He decided to buy an island in a beautiful, scenic environment. He could afford the entire island, and he wanted to enjoy his privacy and personal space, so he purchased the whole thing. This pristine island, surrounded by gorgeous blue ocean water with the sound of waves crashing against the shore, was all his.

One day someone gave him a great idea. They mentioned the island was so beautiful that it would make a great location for an elite golf course. His friend told the man that if he built the golf course on his island, it would give him something fun to do. So the man hired a construction crew and built a golf course on his island.

But then a lot of his business partners and friends started hearing wonderful stories about this amazing golf course, and they also wanted to play there. They asked him if they could play, and being a nice man, he agreed. But then they encouraged him to build a hotel so they would have a place to stay, pointing out that the hotel could also finance his island for upkeep and future projects. He agreed.

After a while, many people flocked to this island with its magnificent golf course and elite hotel. Others wanted to stay, too, and they looked for places offering a permanent living situation. This caused the man to build a small clinic, houses, and a police department. Later, he added a one-room school.

By the time it was all over, the man could no longer smell the ocean. The air had been densely affected by the construction and people who had come to live there. He had lost the pristine privacy he had originally sought out.

That's how the world is. It wants to crowd out the reason you sought the relationship with Jesus Christ in the first place. It wants to pollute your time and personal space with stuff, people, activities, and interests that draw you away from Him. The world wants to make you forget the peace that is yours in Him. It wants you to respond to the voices of people rather than the still, small voice of the One through whom you have been redeemed and under whom you serve.

In the passage we looked at earlier, 1 John 2:15-17, we read the real deal about the world and what it is we are loving. There are three things he points out, stripping the world of its lure. He calls it the lust of the flesh, the lust of the eyes, and the pride of life. Everything in the world falls into one of these three categories.

The lust of the flesh means to crave and desire pleasure that is outside the will of God, either because the thing itself is wrong or because you are desiring a right thing but in an illegitimate way.

For example, one of the great pleasures of life is eating. It's a necessity but also a pleasure. Yet even though the desire for the pleasure of food is there, the Bible declares gluttony as evil. Likewise, God has provided nature to give us medication for healing and health on many levels. But when that nature is taken to another extreme beyond its original intention, it creates addictions and destruction. The Bible makes it clear that drinking wine is not a sin. Yet drunkenness is evil. Sex is not a sin. Immorality is evil. What Satan does is lure us into falling in love with the pleasure itself so much so that we seek it outside of the boundaries of God's provision.

The lust of the flesh is the pursuit of illegitimate forms of pleasure, while the lust of the eyes involves the illegitimate desire for possessions, status, and prominence. Many who are reading this book are drowning in debt because of the lust of the eyes. The craving for stuff, and what that stuff represents, came ahead of your financial priorities before the Lord. Many cannot even honor God with their money because they are bound to honoring Mastercard, Visa, and American Express instead. Satan loves to stir up the lust of the eyes. It's everywhere we go—advertisements in magazines, online, billboards, and on TV. Everywhere you look someone is telling you that your life will be better if you just get this one more thing. And even though you can't truly afford this one more thing, you go ahead and buy it. That's due to the lust of the eyes. That's how people wind up spending money they don't have to impress people they don't know.

Relying solely on what you see can lead to a loss in what you experience spiritually. You may be too young to remember this, but years ago, the government introduced a new form of payment called the Susan B. Anthony dollar. The Susan B. Anthony dollar deviated from paper money. It put the value of a dollar into a coin. The main issue with this new form of payment, and why it was later suspended from production, was that it felt and looked so much like a quarter. Because of the similarities, people would often confuse the two. While it was worth four quarters, people would spend it like one, shorting themselves of the value they were due.

A believer who seeks after the world lives with a similar level of confusion and its resultant loss. A worldly believer is so immersed in the world's way of thinking that it's as though others can no longer tell if he or she is a quarter or a dollar. In fact, he or she can no longer tell if they are a quarter or a dollar. While the value has been set high by the redemption of Jesus Christ, worldly believers often look more like chump change. In addition, they shortchange themselves in their decisions, thoughts, and conversations. Rather than aligning what they say and do with value prescribed to them by God, they settle. Whether that be in settling for a toxic relationship, or settling for a career rather than a calling, or even settling for short-term monetary bumps over long-term eternal rewards—far too many Christians lower their spiritual value in this life.

Check Off My List

Beyond the lust of the flesh and the lust of the eyes, though, also falls the pride of life. The pride of life involves both these things and more. It is an intentional attempt to focus on self-promotion rather than God-promotion in what you do and say. It also involves your mindset. If your mindset fails to recognize God as the source of all things, you will inevitably fall to the pride of life because you will mistakenly look to yourself as the reason for your own successes. Pride is often measured by checking off a list of achievements and accumulating a certain number of friends, likes or comments, and so on. Lists can lead us down the wrong path.

In fact, a lot of people define *worldliness* with an exclusionary list. They make it all about a "Do Not Do This" list. But making a list doesn't capture the essence of what worldliness is. One problem is that our lists are always too short. Some people will leave off things they enjoy doing while putting things on the list that they don't. Another problem with lists is that sometimes they are also too long. That's what we call legalism. Many believers are bound in legalism, failing to enjoy a multitude of blessings God has given simply because they heard somewhere from someone that those things were somehow sinful.

But the real problem with seeking to define *worldliness* through lists is that it focuses entirely on the external actions, while ignoring the reality that God looks at the heart (1 Samuel 16:7). One could keep all the rules of one's particular code, yet still have a disobedient, rebellious heart toward God.

It's like the second grader who was forced to stand for the roll call in class even though he didn't want to. He had a smile on his face as he stood, which surprised the teacher since she knew he didn't like to stand.

She usually had to threaten him with losing recess to get him to stand. So this time, the teacher asked him why he was smiling, to which he replied, "Because I'm sitting on the inside." In his own way, he had found the avenue to break the rule. Even if it was only in his own mind, that was good enough for him.

The thing about God is that He knows our hearts. He knows if we are just obeying a rule to avoid the consequences, or if we are truly obeying out of a spirit of love and gratitude.

And while God knows the truth of our internal alignment, Scripture also gives us three signs, or manifestations, of worldliness that we can use to help us know the truth of our internal alignment as well.

The first real sign of whether your heart is worldly is your level of conflict with others. A believer who lives in an ongoing state of conflict is revealing a worldly spirit. Scripture shows us that this form of relational interaction stems from the flesh (Titus 3:1-3). Conflicts that have their root in jealousy, selfishness, and even pettiness come from the flesh.

The New Testament gives us plenty of examples of the infighting that occurs when worldliness is allowed to reign. The church at Corinth comes to mind first. The believers there were taking their disputes with one another to secular court, dishonoring the name of Christ (1 Corinthians 6:1-8). They had even turned the Communion table into a source of conflict while boasting about how spiritual they were.

The church at Philippi wasn't much better. Paul had to chide them concerning two women who couldn't seem to get along (Philippians 4:2-3). And in his letter to the Galatians, Paul spoke of them like animals devouring each other in conflict (Galatians 5:15).

At the root of so much worldly-minded conflict is the anger that flares up when things go differently from how we had hoped. Differing from righteous anger (anger against sin or confronting a legitimate problem or dispute), unrighteous anger comes from the flesh within. Its aim is venting; a releasing of pent-up passions disturbed through discouragement, frustration, or irritation. James 1:20 tells us, "For the anger of man does not achieve the righteousness of God."

The Bible is clear: You and I can't accomplish God's work when we're empowered by human anger. That's why we need to be "slow to anger" (James 1:19)—slow to take matters into our own hands in an unbiblical way.

The Bible is also clear that there is to be no division in the body of Christ. The Corinthians I just mentioned were "walking like mere men," and the evidence was "jealousy and strife" among them (1 Corinthians 3:1-3).

Someone might say, "Well, I just have a bad temper." No, you don't have a bad temper. A bad temper has you. You're being controlled by a spirit of worldliness. As long as you are quick to get angry rather than slow to get angry, you aren't going to fix anything because you have removed God from both the equation and the solution. Essentially, you are on your own.

Worldliness results in internal conflict, and that internal conflict is behind conflict with others. The Bible shows us that truth in James 4:1-2: "Is not the source [of conflict] your pleasures that wage war in your members? You lust and do not have; so you commit murder. You are envious and cannot obtain; so you fight and quarrel."

The word *members* here is a reference to a believer's physical body. James is talking about the pleasures that battle internally for control over us. If you're looking at others as the cause of the issues you are facing, you won't find it. The cause is located within you.

The word *pleasures* used in James 4:1 is the root of our English word *hedonism*. Hedonism, the pursuit of pleasure for its own sake, is based totally on self-satisfaction and self-gratification. Thus, until you identify and deal with the conflict within, you will never fix the crisis without.

Think back to the first family on record. Why did Eve commit the first sin in Eden? Scripture teaches that her decision was based on personal pleasure. Eve saw that the fruit was "good," "a delight," and "desirable" (Genesis 3:6). That tree was a "feel good" tree. Eve's pleasures waged war within her, and she lost.

There is a war going on within us, even though we may take it out on others. This war stems from uncontrolled desires within us:

> For men will be lovers of self, lovers of money, boastful, arrogant,
> revilers, disobedient to parents, ungrateful, unholy, unloving,
> irreconcilable, malicious gossips, without self-control, brutal,
> haters of good, treacherous, reckless, conceited, lovers of pleasure
> rather than lovers of God, holding to a form of godliness,
> although they have denied its power. Avoid such men as these.
>
> 2 TIMOTHY 3:2-5

The incredible thing is that these uncontrolled desires are carried out by those who hold to the "form of godliness" we discussed in the previous chapter. This means that it is very easy to live a worldly life while maintaining the facade of being a godly Christian.

One way we refer to that today is living as a "cultural Christian." This is the person who checks in to church to cross it off the list but then proceeds to live their life as they want to. Scripture gives us a very straightforward statement about how we are to interact with people like this. As we saw in verse 5, "Avoid such men as these." Above all else, don't be one either. If you are, not only will you experience internal and external conflict, but you will also position yourself so that God is your enemy rather than your friend.

Loving the world always translates into conflict with God. It's spiritual adultery at the highest level, breaking the covenant of fellowship that God secured for you through the death of His Son, Jesus Christ. And while that may be difficult for us to understand, it isn't as difficult to comprehend when we put it in human terms. Take, for example, a husband and wife.

What if this husband were to bring another romantic interest with them to dinner so that it was the three of them there? Do you think the wife would sit idly by and eat her dinner? Neither do I. Rather, she would rightfully storm out because the intimate bond of their relationship would have been violated.

Just as this action would devastate a marriage relationship, when we bring the world's viewpoint, desires, and values into our relationship with God, it creates distance between us. When you as a believer let yourself be compromised by the world, you put yourself in a position of hostility toward God.

We don't speak of this often, but God is a jealous God. It evokes anger in Him when you give your heart to another. James 4:5 tells us, "Or do you think that the Scripture speaks to no purpose: 'He jealously desires the Spirit which He has made to dwell in us'?" There is no room for a rival in your relationship with God. It grieves Him when our attention goes elsewhere, or when we look to other things or people to give direction to our life.

If you and I are going to live with a kingdom focus in our daily lives, God must not only trump the world's attachment to us, but God must always be *first*. He must be our priority.

This thing of priority matters because there are certain things God cannot do. For example, God cannot lie. Neither can He sin. But there is another thing God cannot do. He won't allow Himself to be in second place, or even lower than that, in your life or in the lives of His followers. The Bible regularly tells us about the jealousy of God (Exodus 20:5; 34:14; Deuteronomy 4:24; 32:16; Joshua 24:19; Psalm 79:5). This jealousy is rooted in His character and His commitment to us. Because of who God is, He demands and deserves priority in our lives.

We must learn to recognize when first love has turned to second love (or worse) in our lives as illustrated in Revelation 2:4: "But I have this against you, that you have left your first love."

How do we know when the world has usurped God's rightful place in our hearts and that the accusation in Revelation 2:4 is apt for us? One way is whenever performance for God becomes an end in itself. Whenever I preach simply to preach, rather than preaching out of a heartfelt love and devotion to the Lord, I have turned my focus to the world. Whenever you spend time in your daily devotions just to check it off your list, you have shifted your focus to the world.

God knows everything, and He especially knows when we are pursuing a performance rather than pursuing Him. It is possible in the Christian walk to go through a program and a process, all the while missing the Person. This is because if a relationship is based on a checklist, there is a problem in that relationship. In fact, this devolves into living the Christian life by law rather than by grace (Galatians 5:4).

Unfortunately, far too many believers live this way. They assume that to be a good Christian, they need to do this, that, and the other, while avoiding this, that, and the other. When they have their list completely checked off, they think the Lord must be happy with them. The biblical story of Martha and Mary sheds light on this. If you remember the story, you know that Martha is busy in the kitchen cooking up a full meal. During this time, Mary is sitting at Jesus' feet, enjoying an intimate relationship with Him. Read Luke 10:38-42 if you are not familiar with this account.

Seeing Mary sitting while she is working, Martha comes out and complains to Jesus. She wants to know why He is spending time talking with Mary rather than telling her to help fix the meal. Martha is so upset with Mary that she isn't even talking to Mary. She could have called her into the kitchen herself to help cook. But instead, she goes directly to Jesus to complain about her.

Do you recall what Jesus says in response? We read it in verses 41 and 42, "But the Lord answered and said to her, 'Martha, Martha, you are worried and bothered about so many things; but only one thing is necessary, for Mary has chosen the good part, which shall not be taken away from her.'"

Jesus tells Martha plainly that He is not going to send Mary into the kitchen to cook. The reason why He is not going to do that is because then He would have two Marthas to deal with. "Only one thing is necessary," He tells her. And that "one thing" is being with Him. In other words, a casserole would do if it would free Martha to come spend time with Him as well.

A lot of us have a list of things not to do, as we looked at earlier on the subject of "worldliness." But we also have our good list of things "to do," which we feel will make us righteous. These are things we are doing for God. But when it comes to lists, we often only have a very short list of how we are seeking to deepen our relationship with God.

Yet whenever devotion to the relationship leaves, the relationship is in trouble. God doesn't want just our programming; He wants our passion. He wants the fire.

For a fire to stay hot in the fireplace, there must be an ongoing, intimate connection between the logs. Once that connection disappears, so does the fire. It doesn't matter if you have a million matches at that point; the fire may light, but it will soon disappear. To keep a fire burning, the logs must be intimately connected. The logs keep each other hot.

This is similar to how many people approach their relationship with God. They seek to get lit with a match. Maybe that is by coming to church and singing worship songs, but by the time they hit the parking lot, the fire is gone. Their spiritual vitality is gone because what had started as a relationship with God has devolved into a ritual. What had started as intimacy drifted into activity. They lost their fire.

When duty replaces devotion, you have shifted your focus to a fatal attraction for the world. Devotion is meant to transform duty into something desirable, done out of a heart of love and generated by a relationship rooted in the primacy of intimacy.

It is only when you turn from the world and turn toward God that you are truly living your kingdom calling. And when you do, James goes on to tell us the promise of what will then be yours: "But He gives a greater grace. Therefore it says, 'God is opposed to the proud, but gives grace to the humble'" (James 4:6). If and when you make the pursuit of God your first love, He will open the storehouses of His favor and give you the greater grace that you need to live a victorious life. He will give you more of Himself than you ever even imagined you could have.

It is in humbling yourself under His hand that you access this greater grace. Doing so will give you the power you need to resist the devil and the worldly lure of this life. You will have all you need to experience the divine destiny God has for you.

9

MORE MONEY

A few years ago, we experienced a phenomenon known as a *tetrad*. A tetrad only occurs once in a blue moon. Or rather, a tetrad only occurs once in a *blood* moon. That's because a tetrad is a series of four consecutive total lunar eclipses spread out over a period of time, which usher in four blood moons in a row.

The reason for the term *blood moon* is that in a total lunar eclipse, the sun, moon, and earth are aligned in such a way that the earth blocks any direct sunlight from reaching the moon. The earth's shadow covers the entire moon instead. The same reason our sky turns pink, or reddish, during the sunrise or sunset is the same reason the moon appears red during the total lunar eclipse. The refracted light gives the image of what has become known as a blood moon.

Rather than witnessing the brilliant white light of a full moon on these nights, we see an eerie-looking covering of doom that envelops the earth.

It is far easier to navigate through a dark night with the light of a full moon than it is when the earth casts its shadow. Similarly, it is far easier to navigate through life's dark nights with God's full light upon us than it is when the things of this earth block His brilliance.

One of the benefits of walking in the light of God's full brilliance comes in having the wisdom to make right choices. I'm sure you've stumbled around in the dark from time to time like I have, only to stub your toe on a table or the end of the bed. Who knew there were so many nerve endings in a little toe, which could create that much pain? But that's what walking without illumination will do. It will lead you into things that evoke pain in your life rather than guide you to your intended destination.

Our time together in this book as we explore how to live life with the clarity of an eternal perspective has been designed to shine the light of God's view on all that you do. Whether it's in dealing with relationship choices or emotional struggles, or simply guiding you on how to view the temporal with regard to the eternal, my aim through these pages is to position you for victory.

In this chapter I want to walk you through having a kingdom perspective on your finances. This is an area that causes many of us a tremendous amount of unnecessary grief. God has laid out for us in His Word how we are to view money, and when we apply His precepts and principles to our lives, particularly with regard to money, we experience the freedom that comes from Him.

God's Word has a lot to teach us about this subject. God does not shy away from the issue. Jesus told a number of parables in the New Testament, nearly a third of which deal with the subject of money. One of every ten verses in the New Testament mentions possessions. The Bible contains five hundred or so verses on prayer, and about another five hundred verses on faith. But there are more than two thousand verses in the Bible on money.

Why is this? Because God knows that our view on money is often an accurate thermometer of our spiritual temperature. Just like you are not to stare directly at the sun during an eclipse because it can damage your eyes, if you focus intently on wealth, its brilliance can blind you spiritually.

That's why the Bible instructs us to not let wealth consume us and puff up our view of ourselves, or to let money tempt us to treat other believers according to their wealth or lack of it (James 2:1-4). That's not just bad taste—it's sinful.

In Luke 12, we come upon Jesus' teaching about the Holy Spirit, about how important He is for both time and eternity. During Jesus' teaching, though, someone interrupts Him.

Now, when I preach, I hear people throughout the sermon saying, "Amen" or "Preach it!" or "Tell us more, Pastor!" I hear things of that sort sprinkled throughout the message. Sometimes it will cause me to pause or cause other congregation members to chuckle or respond back. But never does it stop the sermon altogether.

That wasn't the case with Jesus. The person who interrupted His message took Him completely off course. Jesus was busy speaking on the deep theological truths of blaspheming the Holy Spirit when a listener shouted, "Teacher, tell my brother to divide the family inheritance with me" (Luke 12:13). That bold interruption couldn't be further from what Jesus was talking about.

But Jesus didn't break His stride. He went with it, as only He could, with this reply, "Man, who appointed Me a judge or arbitrator over you?" (Luke 12:14). I imagine there were probably a few laughs in the crowd when he said that. Maybe Jesus smiled too.

But then, as His face grew more solemn, He addressed a critical truth with His next words: "Beware, and be on your guard against every form of greed; for not even when one has an abundance does his life consist of his possessions" (Luke 12:15). As He always does, Jesus went straight to the root. He didn't bother with the man's direct request to help him arbitrate a financial issue with his brother. Rather, he addressed the heart behind the matter with a spiritual truth.

This is because when we apply heaven's perspective to earth's realities, we are able to solve earth's realities in the way they ought to be solved.

Jesus took the conversation deeper than the initial question because He knew the heart that was behind the question. He took a man's simple question and turned it into a platform to preach on greed. Jesus is always going to deal with the motivation and not just the information because it is the motivation that reveals the true nature of the issue at hand. The issue wasn't about dividing the inheritance between two brothers. The issue was the level of greed in both brothers' hearts.

Before we go further into this, let me first define *greed*. Greed has nothing to do with how much money you have. It has nothing to do with the size of your bank account, where you live, the clothes you wear, or the car you drive. The amount of money or possessions does not equate to greed. You can be rich and greedy, but you can also be poor and greedy. You can even be middle class and greedy because greed has to do with something beyond money itself. In biblical terms, greed has to do with whether you have placed the physical, tangible things of life ahead of the spiritual.

Greed has to do with alignment. If the shadow of earth's trinkets has eclipsed the light of God's truth, you are greedy.

Greed has to do with whether your pursuit of things blocks your pursuit of God. You are greedy when you love the money that you don't have, or want to have, more than you love the God that you do have. It's when your thoughts and actions go more toward acquiring or desiring stuff than they do toward adoring or desiring God. When God's will for your life becomes second place because the physical trumps the spiritual, you have become greedy.

Greed is all about priorities, not money. What's more is that it comes in all forms. As Jesus said, we are to watch out for "every form" of greed. Because a person can be greedy in a variety of ways. They can be greedy with their emotions, relationships, ambitions, and more. Greed is a state of the heart, not the wallet. In fact, there is even religious greed where the Bible is used to promote a prosperity theology, making God into a genie in a bottle, there to grant us our every wish.

God is not merely a financier. When we treat Him like one, we become guilty of living in a spirit of greed.

Lest there be any misunderstanding, let me say right off that when the Bible speaks against greed, the issue is not how much a person has. God's primary concern is not how much money you have in the bank, how many cars you have in your garage, or how much tax you have to pay at the end of the year. God's concern is your attitude toward what you have.

Some of God's choicest servants were in fact very wealthy people. Job comes immediately to mind. Satan himself knew that God was the One who enriched Job (Job 1:10). It was true, and God gave Job even more at the end of his life than he had at the beginning (Job 42:10-17). God did not apologize for enriching Job. The Bible says, "It is the blessing of the LORD that makes rich" (Proverbs 10:22). Moses told the Israelites, "It is [God] who is giving you power to make wealth" (Deuteronomy 8:18). So greed is not a matter of how much you have, but instead, it is a matter of how you treat what you have and how you respond to the God who gave it to you.

A greedy person is someone who has taken gold and turned it into a god.

We are heading toward the sin of greed when we start looking at God's blessings as an end in themselves, instead of as a God-given opportunity to serve His eternal purposes. When you look at what God has given you and somehow decide that this has all come about by your own ability— when you see no relationship between God's goodness and the resources you have—you are on dangerous ground.

The sin of covetousness is listed in the Bible alongside some other sins you might be surprised to see it near: drunkenness, murder, swindling, and homosexuality (1 Corinthians 5:11; 6:9-10). Not a very nice list, is it? The Bible puts greed in the same neighborhood as these others because all sin is disobedience and rebellion against God. The sins of greed and covetousness also link to the sin of pride. Pride essentially states that what God has provided is not good enough—and pride, simultaneously, causes you to neglect to be grateful for what He has given.

It's very telling that when God told Moses to tell Pharaoh to let His people go, as we read in the book of Exodus, He specifically said to let them go to the wilderness to worship Him. We read in Exodus 7:16, "You shall say to him, 'The LORD, the God of the Hebrews, sent me to you, saying, "Let My people go, that they may serve Me in the wilderness."'" God wasn't sending His people directly to the land flowing with milk and honey. He said first they must connect with Him in the wilderness. They must get their priorities straight before entering the Land of Promise. He wanted to take them where they would depend on Him for water and manna because He knew the heart of humanity and how quickly it rotates toward that which it can see, to worship it instead of the one, true God.

Knowing God deeply is a prerequisite to experiencing and enjoying His blessings because if you skip God and go directly to the blessings, you may become so enthralled with the blessings that you forget the One who gave them. God does not mind you having a Promised Land as long as you do not forget Him when you get there. It is in our dependence upon God that we become bonded to His rightful place in our hearts. We see His heart's desire for our focus to be on Him in what He told the Israelites when they reached the Promised Land:

> You shall remember all the way which the LORD your God has
> led you in the wilderness these forty years, that He might humble
> you, testing you, to know what was in your heart, whether you
> would keep His commandments or not. He humbled you and
> let you be hungry, and fed you with manna which you did not
> know, nor did your fathers know, that He might make you
> understand that man does not live by bread alone, but man lives
> by everything that proceeds out of the mouth of the LORD.
>
> DEUTERONOMY 8:2-3

It is easy to get confused on where to focus between what is the Source of all things and the things themselves. When life has plenty, the plenty can become a priority. Because we are spirit beings living in physical bodies, the tendency to rely upon that which we can feel, see, taste, touch, and smell to inform our life choices often outweighs what we can spiritually discern. It is only when we experience lack in our lives that we often look to God, which is why He tested the Israelites in the wilderness. He humbled them to the point where they would know He is their source.

If the Israelites had not sinned before God but rather entered the Promised Land on the original timetable, they may have wound up glorying in their own strength. They may have experienced great wealth quickly and, as a result, made idols of the fruit of the land. Even in the wilderness, they melted their gold and turned it into a calf. Can you imagine what they would have done when blessed in the Promised Land? It was only through a prolonged dependence upon God as they wandered for years that their hearts were humbled and became in tune with His perspective—His kingdom focus.

No one would accuse the grumbling Israelites of greed when all they were looking for was their next meal in the wilderness. But that's because we've defined *greed* by our culture's terms and not by God's. Greed takes all forms, but the root of it is an eclipsing of God's rightful rule in our lives by that which is tangible.

Greed can even show up in your work. Are you more dedicated to the boss than you are to God? Are you more concerned with the bottom line or surpassing your benchmarks than you are with spending time with the Lord Himself? Are you more concerned with your professional profile or platform than with expanding God's kingdom on earth? All these things fall under the header of greed when they block the light of God's place in your heart and in your desires.

When your pursuit of promotion in this world order pushes God to the sidelines, greed has covered your soul.

There are a couple of ways you can know if you have crossed the line into greed. If you are spending more time complaining than you are giving thanks, then you are on the pathway of greed. Or if you spend more time talking about what you don't have rather than what you do, that is also an indicator that you are living with a heart of greed.

Contentment is a great indicator of a spirit in surrender to God's rule and a heart in alignment with a kingdom focus. Contentment is a learned trait though. It goes against our natural tendencies to gravitate toward more, bigger, better, and faster. The apostle Paul writes about it, "Not that I speak from want, for I have learned to be content in whatever circumstances I am" (Philippians 4:11). He doesn't say that he *is* content. Rather, he writes that he has "learned" to be content.

Contentment is a discovery. It's a process of learning how to be at ease with where you are and what the Lord has provided to you. It is the ultimate act of trust in God's sovereignty and provision. Contentment honors God like little else can because it demonstrates faith on both a heart and physical level. It also demonstrates that you are living mindful of eternity, with an understanding that the things of this earth are temporary, and thus should have only a slight hold on your attention.

Contentment is a form of godliness that can produce great gains in your life. We looked at this earlier in another chapter, but it is worth revisiting here in more depth with regard to money. When the apostle Paul wrote to Timothy in one of his letters, he explained it this way:

> But godliness actually is a means of great gain when accompanied
> by contentment. For we have brought nothing into the world,
> so we cannot take anything out of it either. If we have food and
> covering, with these we shall be content. But those who want to
> get rich fall into temptation and a snare and many foolish and
> harmful desires which plunge men into ruin and destruction.
> For the love of money is a root of all sorts of evil, and some by
> longing for it have wandered away from the faith and pierced
> themselves with many griefs.
> I TIMOTHY 6:6-10

Paul didn't write that money itself is evil. He let us know in this passage that it is the love of money which is the root of evil.

When we esteem the value of money over the values of the kingdom of God, we open the door for destruction. In thinking that we are gaining something by pursuing money, we are actually losing. We experience true, lasting gains when we put God and His kingdom first in our lives.

People who have a master's degree sometimes want to go and earn their doctoral degree because a Ph.D. is considered the top of the line in a particular field. But there are also financial benefits to earning a doctorate, and most people who go to all that work don't do it just to have the title after their name. Their value in the marketplace is enhanced—or at least it should be—when they earn a doctorate. Likewise, pursuing godliness—not just remaining content with stagnation in your spiritual life—produces opportunities for you to gain spiritually. One of the great gains of godliness is the wisdom it provides in discerning the effects of the love of money on a person's life. Money, in and of itself, is not evil. It is the love of money that is the root of all sorts of evil.

The temptations that arise when the pursuit of money becomes one of the highest aims are legion. Living with the world's perspective on money has the tendency to lead us away from the faith rather than toward it.

Paul says that instead of loving money and what it can do for us when we are considered to be rich, we are to be rich in serving others. He writes in 1 Timothy 6:18-19, "Instruct them to do good, to be rich in good works, to be generous and ready to share, storing up for themselves the treasure of a good foundation for the future, so that they may take hold of that which is life indeed." The antidote to greed is not poverty. The antidote to greed is giving.

Paul guides us to think with a giving mindset in this passage, helping us see the importance of a kingdom focus. It is in being rich in good works that we store up for ourselves that which will last—treasures in eternity. I understand that this sits in stark contrast to the mindset the world seeks to conform us to, but that's why we are called to "renew our minds" according to the Spirit and not be molded by the world (Romans 12:2).

In cultivating a spirit within you by renewing your mind so that you are generous and ready to share all that you have with whomever may need it, you are aligning yourself with the Spirit. You are also being strategic in how you spend your time and energy on earth. This matters because what you send forward into eternity is what you get to keep. You do not get to keep that which you store up down here.

This truth was stated clearly for us in the mini-sermon-in-a-sermon Jesus delivered in Luke 12. You'll recall that He was interrupted during his sermon by the man who asked Him to solve his inheritance dispute with his brother. After giving some stern warnings on greed, Jesus then delivered a mini sermon of sorts when he told a parable about a wealthy man who had a number of storage units packed with his grains and his goods:

> The land of a rich man was very productive. And he began
> reasoning to himself, saying, "What shall I do, since I have no
> place to store my crops?" Then he said, "This is what I will do:
> I will tear down my barns and build larger ones, and there I
> will store all my grain and my goods. And I will say to my soul,
> 'Soul, you have many goods laid up for many years to come; take
> your ease, eat, drink and be merry.'" But God said to him, "You
> fool! This very night your soul is required of you; and now who
> will own what you have prepared?" So is the man who stores up
> treasure for himself, and is not rich toward God.
>
> LUKE 12:16-21

The man Jesus spoke of in the parable was a productive entrepreneur. He had successfully calculated his gains and losses. And yet despite his skills, knowledge, and careful planning, he made one very drastic miscalculation in the midst of all of it. This miscalculation was concerning his own retirement, and it involved an assumption.

The man had assumed he would get to retire.

But when the time came for him to sit back and enjoy the spoils of his labor, it was too late to do so. He was ready to party, but his time on earth was over. He was doing what so many people do today. They push God to the side and focus on securing their own future.

Yet none of us are guaranteed a future. None of us are even guaranteed a tomorrow.

To store up treasures for yourself while excluding God from the equation is risky business. When you leave God's kingdom focus out of your plans, you have no guarantees of what you will be walking into. It's not wrong to make plans, it's just unwise to make them without a view for eternity and God's rightful rule over your life.

Jesus didn't condemn the fact that the businessman in the parable was working hard. He didn't say that it was sinful to want to enjoy the fruits of his labor. No, His concern came in that the man sought to do all that apart from God.

It's easy to exclude a kingdom focus when you are always trying to make some deadline. It's easy to focus on what we can see and how our own efforts impact the bottom line. But what we must keep in mind is that everything we do has its root in God. The businessman in Jesus' parable had a very productive land. But he forgot that he didn't make the land. God did. So the very system that he was building his productivity on depended first and foremost on God providing it. It also depended on God giving the rain to nourish it, as well as the sun to strengthen it.

Similarly, all that you do is rooted in God as the source. That's why it is critical to keep a kingdom focus. A kingdom focus is an honest focus, acknowledging that the Giver of all good things is God. There is no such thing as productivity without God. That's why perspective is so important:

Come now, you who say, "Today or tomorrow we will go to such
and such a city, and spend a year there and engage in business
and make a profit." Yet you do not know what your life will be
like tomorrow. You are just a vapor that appears for a little while
and then vanishes away. Instead, you ought to say, "If the Lord
wills, we will live and also do this or that." But as it is, you boast
in your arrogance; all such boasting is evil.

JAMES 4:13-16

Leaving God out of the planning leaves you on your own. Including
God in the planning means you are living with a kingdom focus. Your
time, talents, and treasures are being used in the best possible way for
His goals and agenda. In doing so, you are then storing up treasures
in heaven that neither moth nor rust will destroy. You are maximizing
all that God has given you in such a way that brings Him glory and
others good.

One of the main ways for overcoming greed in your life involves this
idea of where you lay up your treasure. Jesus tells us how to do this:

Do not store up for yourselves treasures on earth, where moth
and rust destroy, and where thieves break in and steal. But store
up for yourselves treasures in heaven, where neither moth nor
rust destroys, and where thieves do not break in or steal; for
where your treasure is, there your heart will be also.

MATTHEW 6:19-21

Jesus is telling us not to get too focused on earthly wealth because it
will all eventually pass away. None of it will transfer to heaven. When
we think about our money and possessions, we need to think in terms of
using what God has given us to advance His kingdom agenda and to help
bring more people to Him.

But if the treasures that you seek to have on earth are only for your personal purposes or pleasures and not somehow linked with eternity, then your heavenly bank account will be low when you get there. Only what you do for eternity gets sent ahead.

Another way to overcome the spirit of greed in your life and live with a kingdom focus is by openly and continually acknowledging that God is the Owner of all you have. Even though you may think you own and control the possessions you have in life, you don't. You can't control what happens to them. You can't keep the rust and moths from taking their toll. Thieves may come in and steal all you have. The stock market may take a plunge and deplete the savings you've been counting on all along.

But if you are viewing your money and possessions with a kingdom focus and optimizing your life on earth to lay up heavenly treasures, then God's name is being glorified and He will take care of you. God doesn't allow moths or thieves to mess with His things. He doesn't let inflation or recession upset His plans. Stock markets don't determine what happens to His possessions.

This is why I encourage believers to dedicate not only their children but also their homes and cars and everything else to God and His kingdom. I invite them (and you) to say, *Everything I have, including my family and my very self, is Yours. And since everything I have is Yours, Lord, I'm not going to worry about it because I know You can take care of Your things better than I can. Use it for Your glory.* When this takes place, not only will your personal life improve through a greater focus toward kingdom values and goals, but you will also help support the advancement of God's kingdom agenda.

This cure for greed is crucial because, as we read just a little bit ago, "where your treasure is, there your heart will be also" (Matthew 6:21). Now I don't want you to miss this important precept in what the Scripture teaches. It would seem logical to say that our treasure will follow our hearts. It would seem to make sense to say that we will spend our money on the things we love. But Jesus said just the opposite. He said that you will come to love what you spend your money on—so be careful where you put your money. Let me give you an example of this.

Suppose you were sitting in church listening to your pastor's sermon when someone came to you and whispered that your house was on fire. Chances are your heart would race, and you'd get up and leave immediately. Why? Because your most valuable possessions were being threatened.

Of course, there's nothing wrong with rushing to your home if it's on fire. My point is simply that your heart is tied to your home because so much of your time, talents, and treasures are tied up there too. Your heart follows your treasure, so make sure you are investing in things of eternal value.

Now let me drive this point home. How many times have you told yourself that since things are tight this week, you really don't have any money to spare for your giving? Why is it that when things are tight, it's always the Lord's money that gets left out?

Are you like the farmer who had two prize-winning calves? He decided to give one to the Lord and keep one for himself. One day one of the calves died, and the farmer told his wife, "Honey, something awful happened. The Lord's calf just died."

In Psalm 62:10 we find wise words for those of us who want to live with a kingdom focus: "If riches increase, do not set your heart upon them." Friend, it's okay to prosper; just don't let your heart be enraptured by the tangible blessings God allows you to *have*. Let God capture your heart and keep it, as you keep your focus on Him.

10

THE PAYOFF

When we were starting out as a fairly new church over forty years ago, we had purchased a small A-frame building sitting on two acres of land, nestled amid undeveloped land as far as the eye could see. This building served as our church for several years. And while God had impressed upon me—even back then—that we would one day own all the land on both sides of the street, we only owned two acres at this time.

The first path to expansion involved an adjoining piece of land that housed a day care center. It was a popular day care center, and the owner didn't appear to be in any mindset to move. Over time, though, the pull of a sale became more alluring to him as he witnessed our parking lot becoming fuller and fuller each Sunday. He knew that we were growing beyond our capacity to hold. He also knew that we had our hearts set on his building and land. Thus, he approached the proposed sale as any businessman would.

He raised the price.

High.

And while we were a growing church, we were still just a struggling church situated in an urban part of town. The contributions that came in barely covered our bills. Paying the very hiked price for the building next door was simply out of the question. We didn't have those kinds of funds.

But knowing who our source was, I sought Him for the land anyhow. After all, this was God's vision He had placed in my heart. This was His church, not mine. If He wanted us to acquire the land with the building next door, He would provide the way for that to happen. It was as simple and straightforward as that. So I turned it over to the Lord in prayer, and I let it go.

You know, your life can be as simple and straightforward as that too. When you live with the mindset of a kingdom focus, you don't have to manipulate, maneuver, or create makeshift solutions to address the issues you face. Living with a kingdom focus sets you free to soar to the heights He's planned for you. It takes the pressure off you to perform, cause things to happen on your own, or achieve the visions He's placed in your heart. They are His visions, after all. Why not rely on Him to produce them. Living with a kingdom focus allows you to rest, knowing that the God who created the universe is big enough to handle whatever it is you might be facing as well.

Long story short, a few months after I turned the situation over to the Lord in prayer and released my concern toward how we would acquire the land, a situation took place that significantly affected the owner of the day care. Not long after, the owner showed up at our church wanting to talk to me. He had decided to reduce the price of the building and the land so that he could move to another location quickly. God gave us the ability to make the purchase based on this drastically lowered amount.

This is just the sort of thing that God does, has done, and continues to do for those who place their hope in Him, aligning their thoughts, emotions, and decisions underneath both His rule and His care. In fact, God can even use a thief to accomplish His plans. Which is why we should never box God into our own solutions. He is so much bigger than what we can even imagine. Learning to trust Him and rest in His care is the most liberating thing you can ever do. It will position you for success and victory in every area of your life.

We've spent the bulk of our time together in these pages discussing what it means to live with a kingdom focus and why you should commit to a shift in your thinking in order to carry that out. But I want to close our time together with an important reminder of one of the greatest benefits that comes when you choose to live this way. In our day and age of worry, anxiety, fear, and uncertainty, this benefit is priceless. It belongs to all of us, yet it is accessed by only a few. Jesus purchased it for each of us but only those who truly embrace a mindset of His kingdom receive it.

It is the benefit known as *rest*.

Calm.

Trust.

The assurance of security.

The profit of peace.

Birds and Ball Games

Jesus had just wrapped up teaching on discipleship truths aimed at the religious leaders of His day when He turned His attention toward the general public. He changed the subject to an issue everyone struggles with to some degree or another. Maybe He could feel the collective worry in the hearts of those around Him. Maybe He could intuit their tenseness. Perhaps He sought to relieve the stress so many carried on their shoulders; stress that had chiseled on their foreheads over time. Whatever the case, He changed His message from one geared more toward rebuke to one aimed solely at offering comfort. He went from teaching on holiness to encouraging hope.

More than twelve verses are dedicated to this portion of Jesus' message. Coming at the same issue through several different illustrations, He resembled a tent preacher at a big crusade, saying the same thing in enough different ways for those listening to understand. That's how badly Jesus wanted them—and wanted us by virtue through them—to comprehend this. To grasp it. To live according to the freedom found through applying it.

What is the bottom line of everything He said that day? If and when you live your earthly life with a kingdom focus, you will never have to worry again. At all.

If you've been a Christian for any length of time, you've probably read this passage before. But let's look at Jesus' teaching in its entirety as it sets the stage for this all-encompassing truth:

> For this reason I say to you, do not be worried about your life,
> as to what you will eat or what you will drink; nor for your
> body, as to what you will put on. Is not life more than food,
> and the body more than clothing? Look at the birds of the air,
> that they do not sow, nor reap nor gather into barns, and yet
> your heavenly Father feeds them. Are you not worth much
> more than they? And who of you by being worried can add a
> single hour to his life? And why are you worried about clothing?
> Observe how the lilies of the field grow; they do not toil nor do
> they spin, yet I say to you that not even Solomon in all his glory
> clothed himself like one of these. But if God so clothes the
> grass of the field, which is alive today and tomorrow is thrown
> into the furnace, will He not much more clothe you? You of
> little faith! Do not worry then, saying, "What will we eat?" or
> "What will we drink?" or "What will we wear for clothing?"
> For the Gentiles eagerly seek all these things; for your heavenly
> Father knows that you need all these things. But seek first His
> kingdom and His righteousness, and all these things will be
> added to you.
>
> So do not worry about tomorrow; for tomorrow will care for
> itself. Each day has enough trouble of its own.

MATTHEW 6:25-34

The takeaway point: Don't worry. Just don't do it.

Yes, I understand there are a lot of things in our world about which to worry. We worry about our finances, careers, health, age, terrorism, the stock market, relationships, and more. We worry about what other people think about us. How many people liked our post or image on social media. We worry about how we look. What we wear. And who is even going to notice. Some of our worries are trivial. Some are critical.

If we were to perform an assessment on whether there exist valid items about which to worry, we would undoubtedly walk away from that assessment saying, "Yes, there are. In this world, yes, there are."

And yet in the face of this reality that we all seem to face, Jesus had the audacity to come on the scene and tell you and me not to worry at all.

Did Jesus know how deep our worries went? Did He realize that worry in and of itself has turned into a major medical issue in our day and age? We've given it sophisticated names now such as obsessive-compulsive disorder, panic attacks, post-traumatic stress disorder, phobias, anxiety, and much more. It rears its ugly head in all forms and fashions. It is the monster crawling around in our minds that won't allow us to rest, keeping us up at night or chained to pills that help us sleep.

Worry pays the salaries of countless counselors in our nation. It is interest paid on trouble before it's due, or even when it will never be due at all. Roughly 80 percent of the things people worry about never happen. Even so, worry has become a multibillion-dollar industry, ballooning the reach of pharmaceutical lines like never before in all history.

And yet Jesus stated plainly (as seen in my Tony Evans's translation), "Stop it! Don't worry!"

The Greek word used for "worry" in Jesus' message to us came from the concept of being strangled or choked. It makes sense because that's what worry seems to do—it chokes us and prevents us from functioning to the fullest. Worry leaves us frustrated when we ought to be free. For any football fans, worry tells you to take a knee in an AFC Championship game that has only fifty seconds left before the half ends and two time-outs in your pocket, with an only four-point lead. Worry affects behavior, crippling those who have it and keeping them from reaching their highest potential in life.

Which is why Jesus said that if you are His disciple, then you should stop it.

To worry is to focus on the wrong thing. It is to honor the wrong authority. It is to question God's very integrity. Jesus said that the Gentiles—the pagan people who did not know God—were concerned with the things that produce worry. But that God's people who know Him and have a relationship with Him should not live or think the same way as those who do not. I can imagine that God is insulted by our worry. He knows that it dominates us in such a way that it impedes our ability to function as children of the King ought to function.

As Jesus pointed out in His many illustrations on the subject, God values us more than even the birds and the flowers. He is our Creator and our caring Father. The birds do not sow or reap, they do not plant their food and harvest it, yet they manage to eat every day. How? Because our heavenly Father feeds them.

If our Father feeds birds that have no eternal soul, how much more will He take care of you and me? It's a rhetorical question. I don't expect you to answer it. Here's another one: Would someone keep a bird feeder stocked full, but then neglect to feed their own kids?

God feeds the birds, yet they have no eternal value to Him. You have so much value to Him that He gave His only Son to purchase your salvation and redemption from hell. Think about that for a moment. Then take another moment to think about the ravens.

For those familiar with Scripture, you know that the Gospels were written by four different people: Matthew, Mark, Luke, and John. And just as there would be a variety of takes on the same exact story if you and I were to witness a similar event together, the Gospels also frequently tell the same story but with the emphasis that stood out to the person recording it.

In the book of Matthew, for example, Matthew writes that Jesus said to look at the "birds" of the air. But in the book of Luke, Luke specifically said that Jesus mentioned the ravens (see Luke 12:24). Now, Luke was a physician by trade. His mind was predisposed to details and the importance of keeping those details. Matthew, on the other hand, was a former tax collector. A raven was just a bird to him.

The reason I bring up this distinction is because Jesus intentionally chose to direct the attention of His listeners to a bird that was considered "unclean" at that time. Ravens had been designated as "unclean" animals, which the Jewish people were to avoid having any contact with, let alone eating.

The point is that Jesus asked His Jewish disciples to consider a bird they were told to never consider. In that stark contrast, He was asking them to realize that if God would provide for this "unclean" bird, He would surely provide for them. If God would care so deeply and so sufficiently for something He Himself declared as "unclean," wouldn't He care for His own children—His own followers—even more? Are we really to think that God has less concern for our needs than He does for a raven, a bird He had once designated as "off-limits" to His people?

When a raven cannot find a worm, you do not see the raven developing an ulcer, scratching its head, and flopping down in despair. What does the raven do when it can't find a worm? The raven simply flies to another location to look for a worm someplace else. There is no need for birds to get all shook up because all birds assume the same thing: The Creator values them enough to provide for them.

It is only when you and I do not understand what the ravens understand that we get shook up in the absence of what we think we may need at that moment. When one of our resources starts to run dry, we worry. That is, unless we live our lives with a kingdom focus that understands that God is not limited by resources or the lack thereof. He has promised to supply when you live under His overarching rule.

He is your source. What's more, He is your *only* source. You do not have many sources. What you have are resources—mechanisms that God uses to provide for you. But God is your *only* source. When you truly understand and embrace this truth, you will be set free from worry's stranglehold on you. When you are completely focused on Him, you are no longer distracted by the failures and misgivings of the resources you once looked to. You are no longer defined by what others do. You will discover that in looking to God and casting your gaze squarely on Him, you will be able to see beyond what you can see right now and even beyond what others may see. Or even beyond what others may *say*.

After all, much of our worry stems from the pressure placed on us by our culture, friends, families, coworkers, and more. A large part of the stress and anxiety plaguing us has grown out of the comparison trap set by the social media mindset of our day. But when we look to God as our only source, we will discover the freedom to soar. Just like ravens soar. Just like eagles soar—or even just like *an* Eagle soared in the NFL playoffs a few years ago.

His name is Torrey Smith. He wore number 82. Most of you reading this book have probably never heard of him. He wasn't a superstar with superstar stats. He is a former NFL player, one of many who have gone through the ranks only to live out the rest of their lives in obscurity. He is also a husband and a father. And he was an Eagle, too, of the Philadelphia Eagles.

I'm not writing to you right now about Smith because he caught a lot of passes. He actually didn't catch that many. But I am writing because of two passes he did catch with the Eagles, at just the right moments. Kind of like he did a few years earlier while playing for another bird—the Baltimore Ravens.

It was the first quarter of Super Bowl 47 when the Ravens faced the 49ers in a game most people thought the 49ers would win. The Ravens were a wild-card team, having done what few had ever done before then or since. They had beaten Timeless-Tom Brady and the Patriots in their own house to advance past the AFC Championship Game. That alone was considered a major victory. But the Ravens wanted more. Despite what others said, they thought they could win the whole thing.

A few minutes into the game, Ravens quarterback Joe Flacco threw a pass that was a bit too high—one commentator said he threw it too high even as the ball drifted through the air. But somehow, someway, Smith donned his wings and flew up to grab it straight out of the sky. The completed long pass set the Ravens up for a touchdown just a few plays later. That touchdown not only became a momentum setter against the team most people had called to win, but it also served as the difference-maker in the final score, with the Ravens going on to win by only three points.

Smith's catch stood out from the others to most viewers at that time perhaps because of what we had all witnessed earlier in the year. On the road to the playoffs, the Ravens faced the Patriots in a previous game. The game had taken place at the start of the season but also at the end of a life.

It was Smith's younger brother, Tevin, who had been tragically killed in a motorcycle accident less than twenty-four hours before the Ravens–Patriots game began. And while the Ravens' ownership gave Smith the opportunity to sit out of the game and not play, he chose instead to play it in honor of his brother's memory and life. It was an honor that Smith made good on by catching six passes for 127 yards, including a touchdown with only four minutes left in the game. This touchdown brought the Ravens to within two points of the Patriots, which the Ravens then went on to eclipse with a field goal. The Ravens won that game by only one point, and Smith won the hearts of viewers everywhere.

So when he flew up to catch that pass in the Super Bowl so many months later, it was more than just a pass to set up a touchdown for most of us watching. It was also an exclamation point on a tribute to a brother taken away far too soon.

Yet glory fades and trophies get placed on mantles out of sight. A new season starts. Teams trade players. And soon Smith was no longer a Raven anymore. But soon another bird came calling his name. They gave him the same number but a new color and a new team for which to play: the Eagles.

Finding himself in a new round of Divisional and Championship games once again, Smith continued to soar. Despite the naysayers throughout the season who had said he hadn't lived up to their expectations, he knew who he was. He knew what he could do. He knew just how to rest in the reality of truth.

"I'm not worried at all," Smith told a reporter shortly before the playoff season began.[2] Having gone seven full games without a catch longer than eleven yards, Smith didn't have many others who shared his conviction. People did worry. Fans did fret. Reporters did judge. They said Smith wasn't living up to their expectations. But he knew better than that. He knew he had been getting open but that the calling of the plays went other ways. And while it would be easy to cower to negativity and the disappointment brought about by unmet expectations in the eyes of others, Smith chose to focus only on what he knew to be true.

Yes, he could have focused on the voices surrounding him. But he chose not to.

You have a choice as well. I understand that choice isn't easy. The voices are loud that clamor for your attention. The pressure is real in life's mounting tensions. But when you choose to focus on what you know to be true—what God's Word says about Him and what it says about you— you, also, don't have to worry. Just like number 82.

It was the Divisional playoff game. The Eagles were underdogs. The other bird, the Falcons, were favored to win. All sixty minutes would be hard-fought, but there was one play that could have changed everything in one moment. It was a bad pass from the Eagles quarterback. Watching it, you might have thought it would be an easy interception, possibly even a runback for a touchdown. A momentum swinger, no doubt. But some-how the ball bounced off the knee of the potential interceptor, ricochet-ing up into the air as Eagles fans everywhere held their collective breath. Flashbacks of the Immaculate Reception in a previous Divisional playoff no doubt washed through the memories of those who then saw the ball somehow land in the hands of the very-ready-and-very-eager Eagles player named Smith.

The Eagles had been trailing up to that point. An interception and runback by the favored Falcons could have proved devastating, to say the least. But in Smith's uncanny ability to remain alert in the face of a play gone bad, he grabbed the floater and flew up the field for a gain. The Eagles would go on to win that match by only five points.

Later, in the Championship game against the also favored other team, the Vikings, Smith took part in an unpracticed and unprecedented play called a flea-flicker. This flea-flicker was so unexpected that even when the quarterback got it called into him as the next exchange, he said he had to "try not to smile. . . . It was my first time, so I had to try not to smile."[3] The play itself went off without a hitch despite having never been run even in practice. The pass to Smith resulted in an incredible leap once again and a catch in the corner of the end zone, as he came to land on the pylon itself. That catch sent the birds up enough to have a comfortable lead going in for the win.

The fans coined the phrase "Fly Eagles Fly" for this Super Bowl run, which is exactly what Smith was able to do. And why was he? Why was a player who had not caught any passes longer than eleven yards in the previous seven games able to put up two amazing plays? All because he had made a choice earlier in the season when the noise of dissenters clanged as raucous chants all around him. He had made the choice not to worry. At all.

The same choice is set before you to make as well. It's your decision. I encourage you to make it. Jesus commands you to make it. Not because difficulties no longer surround you. Nor because disappointments no longer exist. And not because your circumstances have somehow transformed into a cakewalk or a celebration. But rather because you simply make the choice to trust the truth you know. The truth that God cares enough about you to care for you in every way you need Him to.

It is in setting your mind on His eternal perspective, while shifting your focus to His kingdom plan, that you will discover the power of His provision, which will release you to fly. Jesus concludes His message on not worrying with a challenge to seek first the kingdom of God and His righteousness; God will take it from there. It is living with a kingdom mindset that will enable you to soar in this life despite the opposition and challenges that may come your way, as well as to continue to soar in eternity to come.

God has a plan for you. It is a good plan, filled with both a future and a hope. You can make that championship run with Him, but it requires you to set your worry aside, place your focus on High, and keep striving toward His endgame. Never quit. Never throw in the towel. Keep the end in mind, and you will make it through the struggles, the difficulties, and the losses in this life. You can keep going. Keep your eyes on Christ, and you will discover one day when you stand before Him that every moment of your commitment to Him was worth the fight.

Appendix A
THE FOUNDATION OF A KINGDOM FOCUS: ETERNAL SALVATION

The story found in Luke 16:19-31 gives us a glimpse at both sides of the hereafter. We're told about a certain rich man who was dressed in purple and fine linen (very expensive threads!) and lived in luxury every day. He was the envy of everyone. If he were living in modern times, he'd have a Beverly Hills address and his 10,000-square-foot house would be surrounded by manicured lawns and shimmering swimming pools. His staff would attend to his every need. In his driveway, you'd find an exquisite Mercedes-Benz—for use only when the Rolls-Royce was in the shop, or for commuting back and forth to the Learjet. This man was rich beyond imagination and didn't mind letting everyone know it.

The text also tells us about another man—a beggar named Lazarus. Quite the opposite of our rich man, Lazarus depended completely upon others for his very survival.

Not only was this man poor, but he was also sick. His body was covered with open sores that wouldn't heal. His wounds were too infected to close. Besides, the dogs would pass by each day and lick them. Yes, it's a disgusting picture—human misery at its worst.

Poor Lazarus couldn't even beg without help; he had to be laid at the gate of the rich man's home. This was evidently a place with a good deal of foot traffic. After all, you can't beg where there are no people.

But Lazarus had another agenda. We're told that he longed to be fed with the crumbs that fell from the rich man's table. In other words, Lazarus had probably made a contact with a servant from the rich man's household. "Listen, when you take out the garbage, pass by me," he might have said. "Leave the scraps by the gate—they'll be my dinner." Now that is poor.

Eventually, the two men died. Don't miss the significance of that short statement. Both men died. Time has a way of doing that to people, and no one is exempt. The fact is, you are going to die. It doesn't matter how far you jog or how carefully you balance your diet, you are going to die. It makes no difference how healthy you feel, where you live, how much you earn, or who your doctor happens to be. Sooner or later, your time, like mine, will come.

Looking back to our story, the death of the rich man certainly made the headlines. The passing of such a powerful man must have sent ripples through the entire community. Can you imagine the crowd at his funeral? I can almost picture a line of shiny Cadillacs led by a team of motorcycle officers moving traffic to one side.

Lazarus, on the other hand, was likely dropped into a ditch and covered over with dirt.

Nevertheless, make no mistake—despite the enormous differences between them, both men were equally dead.

Becoming aware of our mortality should serve as an incentive to keep our attention focused on eternal goals and values. It reminds us that when our earthly life concludes, our eternal life begins. You see, death is not a period at the end of life's sentence. It is a conjunction, linking time and eternity. The issue at hand is this: How does the sentence read after the conjunction?

A tombstone in a 100-year-old cemetery bears this verse: "Pause, stranger, when you pass me by. As you are now, so once was I. As I am now, so you will be. So prepare for death and follow me."

An unknown visitor added these lines: "To follow you, I'm not content, until I know which way you went!"

It is at this very crossroads that our story takes an interesting turn. Upon Lazarus's death, God dispatched some angels to escort him to the bosom of Abraham. Was this the result of his poverty? No. Because of his suffering? No. It was the fruit of his faith. You see, the name "Lazarus" is a derivative of the name "Eleazar," which means "God has helped." When Jesus told this story of a man named Lazarus, He was not simply describing a man who was poor and sick, but a man whom God had helped.

"Some help," you might say. "He was broke, sick, totally dependent . . . and God didn't even protect him from the dogs. What kind of help is that?"

Jesus wasn't talking about physical deliverance; He was looking deeper. Inside that body of infected flesh was a man whom God had visited in faith. His life in this world was a tragedy, but he knew much about the world to come. Lazarus was a man who knew God.

But what of the rich man? What did his affluence accomplish? We're told that no sooner had he closed his eyes in death than he found himself being tormented in hell. No purgatory, no "sleeping in the grave," no second chances, no options.

Then the formerly rich man did an amazing thing. He looked up and saw Abraham, far away in heaven, comforting Lazarus. There is a remarkable revelation packed into those few short words. You see, the man had eyes—his own eyes. He had a mind—his own mind, with memories and senses intact.

When we die, the essence of life God puts within us (called the soul) is extracted from the body, which can no longer function. At that point, it seems that God transplants our soul into some new frame that, in many ways, is similar to our body. This new frame can see, speak, think, feel . . . it possesses a physical reality.

Want to know how real that reality is? The rich man cried out, "Father Abraham, have mercy on me, and send Lazarus so that he may dip the tip of his finger in water and cool off my tongue, for I am in agony in this flame" (Luke 16:24). The man is on fire, but he is not burning.

All the water in all the oceans couldn't douse those flames. Even so, he begged for the touch of a wet finger as though it would make an eternal difference.

And that's not all. The misery of hell is not only what you feel, but what you see. The rich man had a clear view of heaven. Can you imagine the torture of seeing heaven, but being unable to get near it? How devastating to see friends, loved ones—even enemies—celebrate in the presence of the Lord while you languish in timeless torment.

No wonder the man cried out for pity. Unfortunately, all the sympathy in the world could not help him. Abraham explains,

> Child, remember that during your life you received your good
> things, and likewise Lazarus bad things; but now he is being
> comforted here and you are in agony. And besides all this,
> between us and you there is a great chasm fixed, so that those
> who wish to come over from here to you will not be able, and
> that none may cross over from there to us.
>
> LUKE 16:25-26

Why did God put a "Grand Canyon" between heaven and hell? Why is it that after 20,000 years of torment, you still can't bridge that gap? Why is it that after a million years, you can't get a transfer?

Think back to the book of Genesis. Remember the tree of life? When Adam and Eve sinned, they were put out of the Garden. Angels with flaming swords were posted at the entrance to ensure that they did not find a way to get in and eat from that tree (Genesis 3:24). Had they done so, unregenerate Adam and Eve would have gained access to heaven, and all heaven would be contaminated by sin. Obviously, a sinless God could not allow that to happen. He had to block the door to guarantee it. So a chasm has been established. When you die, you wind up on one side of that abyss forever.

The rich man is now hopelessly stuck on the wrong side. He's left with his affliction and his memories. "Remember . . . ," Abraham said.

In hell, you remember where you went wrong on earth. And the details will be quite specific. The rich man finally realized that his fate was sealed. At that point, his thoughts turned to his loved ones still on earth. "And he said, 'I beg you, father, that you send [Lazarus] to my father's house—for I have five brothers—in order that he may warn them, so that they will not also come to this place of torment'" (Luke 16:27-28).

I have heard people say, "I don't mind going to hell—that's where all my friends will be. It'll be one big party!" Oh, if you could hear from them now. There are no parties, no good times, no friends. There is no love, no peace, no comfort—just screams for mercy. How would you react if you could hear their warnings?

Abraham responded to the rich man's plea: "They have Moses and the Prophets; let them hear them." The rich man knew that his brothers, like himself, had shrugged off the warnings of Scripture. "No, father Abraham," he said, "but if someone goes to them from the dead, they will repent!" Abraham knows better. "If they do not listen to Moses and the Prophets, they will not be persuaded even if someone rises from the dead" (Luke 16:29-31).

"Send a miracle." That's all we want—irrefutable, tangible, visible proof that God is who He says He is. Doesn't that seem logical? I hear it all the time when witnessing to people: "If God will _____ [fill in the blank], then I'll believe!"

The truth is, our lives are jam-packed with miracles and we still don't believe. The intricacy of the human body is a miracle, yet we turn a blind eye toward abortion. The working of the universe is a miracle, yet scientists fail to see the hand of God, clinging instead to a ridiculous theory claiming that nothing plus nothing becomes something.

In John 11:38-44, another man named Lazarus actually does come back from the dead, resurrected by Jesus. Did the Jews repent? On the contrary, they wanted to put Lazarus back in the grave and began planning the death of Jesus as well (John 12:9-11).

As it turns out, Abraham was right. If a person will not listen to the Word, no miracle in the universe will be enough to make him believe. Let's look back at what the Word tells us.

God's Word declares that man's eternal destiny depends on what he does with Jesus Christ. His Word tells us that Jesus Christ is the Son of God, that He became a man, and that He suffered on the cross, died, and rose again to save us from hell. The Word teaches us that as a bee loses its sting, so death lost its sting when it stung Jesus Christ. The Word proclaims that all who come to Christ by faith can live.

Make no mistake. What kept the rich man out of heaven was not his wealth. Nor did poverty alone earn Lazarus a reward. Each had made a choice to believe or not to believe. Each of us faces that same choice.

Because we have the freedom to choose Christ, there is no reason for any human being to go to hell. Still, hell remains our destination until the moment we unconditionally surrender our lives to the Savior.

No other decision in life deserves more attention than this one. Our choice affects not only our life on earth but also our eternal future. And forever is a long, long time.

Imagine draining all the water out of the Pacific Ocean and replacing it with sand. Then build that sand pile higher and higher until it is as tall as Mount Everest. Now picture a bird that flies in every 5,000 years and carries away one grain of sand each trip. When the bird finally returns for the last grain of sand, one second will have ticked by in eternity.

Deuteronomy 30:19-20 says, "I have set before you life and death, the blessing and the curse. So choose life in order that you may live, you and your descendants, by loving the LORD your God, by obeying his voice, and by holding fast to Him."

Take a cue from Lazarus. If you haven't already, choose life by trusting the Lord Jesus Christ as your only Savior from sin. If you would like to know how to do that, I'm going to walk you through a simple outline to explain it. If you are already saved, you may want to read through this to know how to present the gospel to someone else.

The outline that I'm about to walk you through isn't original to me. I did not discover it; I simply expanded upon it. It's called the "Romans Road." Quite simply, by using key passages from the book of Romans, we can outline everything a man or woman needs to know in order to receive salvation in Jesus Christ.

The Problem

For all have sinned and fall short of the glory of God.

ROMANS 3:23

Salvation is *good news*, but it comes to us against a backdrop of bad news. The bad news is this: We are all sinners. Not one man or woman on planet earth—past, present, or future—is without sin.

The Greek word for "sin" literally means "to miss the mark." It describes a bowman who drew back his string, released his arrow, but failed to hit the bull's-eye. Similarly, sin involves missing the target. What is the target? The verse we just looked at tells us: "All have sinned and *fall short of the glory of God*" (emphasis added). Sin is falling short of God's glory—His standard.

To help you understand this concept, I must attack a popular myth maintained by the media, the literary community, and sometimes even the church itself. The fable is that sin can be measured by degree. For many of us, criminals seem like big-time sinners, while those of us who tell little white lies are lightweight sinners. It appears logical to believe that those in county jail have not sinned as seriously as those in the state penitentiary. But sin looks quite different from God's perspective.

In Scripture, sin is not measured by degree. Either we fall short of God's glory, or we don't. Since the entire sin question pivots on this point, let's make sure we understand our target.

The word *glory* has to do with something being put on display—being shown off. Sin is missing the mark, and "the mark" in this case is properly putting God on display. When we view the issue from this perspective, our understanding of sin begins to change. Any time we have ever done anything that did not accurately reveal who and what God is, any time we fail to reflect the character of God, then we have sinned.

The story is told of two men who were exploring an island when, suddenly, a volcano erupted. In moments, the two found themselves surrounded by molten lava. Several feet away was a clearing and a path to safety. To get there, however, they would have to jump across the river of melted rock. The first gentleman was an active senior citizen but hardly an outstanding physical specimen. He ran as fast as he could, took an admirable leap, but traveled only a few feet. He met a swift death in the super-heated lava.

The other explorer was a much younger, more virile man in excellent physical condition. In fact, the college record he set in the broad jump had remained unbroken to that day. He put all his energy into his run, jumped with flawless form, and shattered his own college record. Unfortunately, he landed far short of the clearing. Though the younger man clearly outperformed his companion, both wound up equally dead. Survival was so far out of reach that ability became a non-issue.

Degrees of "goodness" may be important when hiring an employee or choosing neighbors. But when the issue is sin, the only standard that matters is God's perfect holiness. The question is not how you measure up against the guy down the street, but how you measure up to God. God's standard is perfect righteousness, and it is a standard that even the best behaved or most morally upright person still cannot reach.

The Penalty

Therefore, just as sin came into the world through one man,
and death through sin, and so death spread to all men because
all sinned.

ROMANS 5:12, ESV

As you read this passage, you may be thinking, "If sin entered the
world through one man (Adam), it isn't fair to punish the rest of us." Yet
death spread to all men because "all have sinned." We are not punished
simply because Adam sinned, but because we inherited Adam's propensity
to sin and have sinned ourselves.

Have you ever noticed that you don't need to teach your children how
to sin? Can you imagine sitting down with your child and saying, "Here's
how to lie successfully" or "Let me show you how to be selfish"? Those
things come naturally.

Let me illustrate this another way. Have you ever seen an apple with a
small hole in it? If you do, don't eat it. The presence of the hole suggests
that there is a worm in there waiting for you.

Now, most people don't know how the worm managed to take up
residence in that apple. They think he was slithering by one day when he
decided to bore through the outer skin of the fruit and set up house inside.
However, that is not what happens. Worms hatch from larvae dropped on
the apple blossom. The blossom becomes a bud, and the bud turns into
fruit. The apple literally grows up around the unborn worm. The hole is
left when the worm hatches and digs his way out.

In the same way, the seed of sin is within every one of us at birth.
Though it may take some time before the evidence of sin shows on the
surface, it is there and eventually it makes its presence known.

Sin demands a penalty. That penalty, according to Scripture, is death.

That means physical death (where the soul is separated from the body) and spiritual death (where the soul is separated from God).

The Provision

> But God demonstrates his own love toward us, in that while we
> were yet sinners, Christ died for us.
>
> ROMANS 5:8

Two very powerful words when put together are *but God*. Those words can revolutionize any situation. "My marriage is falling apart. But God . . ." "My husband abandoned us and my children are out of control. But God . . ." "I have no job, no income, and no future. But God . . ." God can restore any situation. He is bigger and more powerful than any life challenge or any predicament with or result from sin.

"I'm a sinner condemned to eternal separation from God. But God . . ." Those same words sum up the Good News for each of us. Even while we were still sinners, God proved His love for us by sending Jesus Christ to die in our place.

How amazing that God would love us so deeply. We have certainly done nothing to deserve it. But the amazement deepens when you consider the significance of Jesus' sacrifice on Calvary.

Because not just anybody could die for the penalty of sin. You see, we all have sinned. So none of us could die to pay the penalty of sin. We each have our own price to pay. Whoever would save us must be perfectly sinless.

Two brothers were playing in the woods one summer day when almost without warning, a bee flew down and stung the older brother on the hand. He cried out in pain. As the younger brother looked on in horror, the bee began buzzing around his head. Terrified, he began screaming,

"The bee's going to get me!" The older brother, regaining his composure, said, "What are you talking about? That bee can't hurt you; he's already stung me."

The Bible tells us that this is precisely what happened on Calvary. God loves you so much that He stepped out of heaven in the person of Jesus Christ and took the "stinger of death" in your place on Calvary. Jesus hung on the cross, not for His own sin, but for my sin and yours. Because Jesus Christ is without sin, His death paid the penalty for all of us.

How do we know that Jesus' death on the cross really took care of the sin problem? Because of what happened on that Sunday morning so long ago. When Mary Magdalene came to Jesus' tomb that morning, she couldn't find Him. She saw someone and thought he was a gardener. She asked him where the Lord's body had been taken. When the gardener turned and removed his cloak, Mary gasped in amazement. It was Jesus.

In fact, according to 1 Corinthians 15:6, over five hundred people personally saw the risen Christ before He ascended into heaven.

I am a Christian today because the tomb is empty. If not for the resurrection, our faith would be empty and useless. As the apostle Paul said, if Jesus were not raised, we should be the most pitied people on earth (1 Corinthians 15:19). But the fact is, Jesus *is* raised. Now what do we do?

The Pardon

If you confess with your mouth that Jesus is Lord and believe in your heart that God raised him from the dead, you will be saved. For with the heart one believes and is justified, and with the mouth one confesses and is saved.

ROMANS 10:9-10, ESV

If good works could save anyone, there would have been no point in Jesus' death. But Jesus knew we couldn't pay sin's price. That's why His sacrifice was vital. In order for His sacrifice to secure our pardon, we must trust in Him for our salvation.

Believing in Jesus means a great deal more than believing about Jesus. Knowing the facts about His life and death is mere "head knowledge." Believing in Jesus demands that we put that knowledge to work. It means to trust, to have total confidence, to "rest your case" on Him. Without knowing, you illustrate this concept every time you sit down. The moment you commit your weight to a chair, you have "believed in" that chair to hold you up. Most of us have so much faith in chairs that, despite our weight, we will readily place ourselves down without a second thought.

If a tinge of doubt creeps in, you might steady yourself by grabbing something with your hand or by keeping your legs beneath you, resting only part of your weight on the chair. That's what many people do with salvation. They're reasonably sure that Jesus is who He said He is. However, they "hedge their bet" by putting some of their trust in their efforts at good behavior, their church traditions, or anything else they can do.

You must understand that if you depend on anything beyond Jesus for your salvation, then what you're really saying is that Jesus Christ is not enough. God is waiting for you to commit the entire weight of your existence to Jesus Christ and what He did on the cross. Your complete eternal destiny must rest upon Him.

You might say, "But my mom was a Christian. And she prayed for me." Praise God. But what about you? Christianity has nothing to do with your heritage. It has nothing to do with the name of the church you attend. It's got to do with whether you have personally placed absolute confidence in the work of Christ alone.

Where Do I Go from Here?

Have you ever confessed your sin to God and trusted in Jesus Christ alone for your salvation? If not, there's no better time than right now.

It all begins with a simple prayer. The exact wording isn't important. What matters is your sincerity. Here's an example:

Dear Jesus, I confess that I am a sinner. I have failed to reflect Your glory and deserve the punishment that results from sin. Jesus, I believe that You are holy and sinless, that You died on the cross at Calvary and rose from the dead to grant salvation. I now place all my confidence in You as my Savior. Please forgive me of my sins and grant me eternal life. Thank You for saving me. I want to live my life for You. Amen.

If you prayed that prayer for the first time, I want to welcome you into the family of God. Also, talk with your pastor or a Christian friend. Let them know about your decision so they can encourage you and help you grow in your newfound faith. Find a church that teaches the Bible and get involved right away. A brand-new focus is up ahead! You have just taken the first step in an amazing, eternal journey.

Appendix B
THE URBAN ALTERNATIVE

The Urban Alternative (TUA) equips, empowers, and unites Christians to impact *individuals*, *families*, *churches*, and *communities* through a thoroughly kingdom agenda worldview. In teaching truth, we seek to transform lives.

The core cause of the problems we face in our personal lives, homes, churches, and societies is a spiritual one; therefore, the only way to address it is spiritually. We've tried a political, social, economic, and even a religious agenda.

It's time for a *kingdom agenda*.

The kingdom agenda can be defined as the visible manifestation of the comprehensive rule of God over every area of life.

The unifying central theme throughout the Bible is the glory of God and the advancement of His kingdom. The conjoining thread from Genesis to Revelation—from beginning to end—is focused on one thing: God's glory through advancing God's kingdom.

When you do not recognize that theme, the Bible becomes disconnected stories that are great for inspiration but seem to be unrelated in purpose and direction. Understanding the role of the kingdom in Scripture increases the relevancy of this several-thousand-year-old text to your day-to-day living, because the kingdom is not only then; it is now.

The absence of the kingdom's influence in our personal lives, family lives, churches, and communities has led to a deterioration in our world of immense proportions:

- People live segmented, compartmentalized lives because they lack God's kingdom worldview.
- Families disintegrate because they exist for their own satisfaction rather than for the kingdom.
- Churches are limited in the scope of their impact because they fail to comprehend that the goal of the church is not the church itself but the kingdom.
- Communities have nowhere to turn to find real solutions for real people who have real problems because the church has become divided, ingrown, and unable to transform the cultural and political landscape in any relevant way.

The kingdom agenda offers us a way to see and live life with a solid hope by optimizing the solutions of heaven. When God is no longer the final and authoritative standard under which all else falls, order and hope leave with Him. But the reverse of that is true as well: As long as you have God, you have hope. If God is still in the picture, and if His agenda is still on the table, it's not over.

Even if relationships collapse, God will sustain you. Even if finances dwindle, God will keep you. Even if dreams die, God will revive you. If God and His rule are still the overarching standard in your life, family, church, and community, there is always hope.

Our world needs the King's agenda. Our churches need the King's agenda. Our families need the King's agenda.

We've put together a three-part plan to direct us to heal the divisions and strive for unity as we move toward the goal of truly being one nation under God. This three-part plan calls us to assemble with others in unity, address the issues that divide us, and act together for social impact. Following this plan, we will see individuals, families, churches, and communities transformed as we follow God's kingdom agenda in every area of our lives. You can request this plan by emailing info@tonyevans.org or by going online to TonyEvans.org.

In many major cities, there is a loop that drivers can take when they want to get somewhere on the other side of the city but don't necessarily want to head straight through downtown. This loop will take you close enough to the city so that you can see its towering buildings and skyline, but not close enough to actually experience it.

This is precisely what we, as a culture, have done with God. We have put Him on the "loop" of our personal, family, church, and community lives. He's close enough to be at hand should we need Him in an emergency but far enough away that He can't be the center of who we are.

We want God on the "loop," not as the King of the Bible who comes downtown into the very heart of our ways. Leaving God on the "loop" brings about dire consequences as we have seen in our own lives and with others. But when we make God, and His rule, the centerpiece of all we think, do, or say, it is then that we will experience Him in the way He longs for us to experience Him.

He wants us to be kingdom people with kingdom minds set on fulfilling His kingdom's purposes. He wants us to pray, as Jesus did, "Not my will, but Thy will be done." Because His is the kingdom, the power, and the glory.

There is only one God, and we are not Him. As King and Creator, God calls the shots. It is only when we align ourselves underneath His comprehensive hand that we will access His full power and authority in all spheres of life: personal, familial, ecclesiastical, and governmental.

As we learn how to govern ourselves under God, we then transform the institutions of family, church, and society using a biblically based kingdom worldview.

Under Him, we touch heaven and change earth.

To achieve our goal, we use a variety of strategies, approaches, and resources for reaching and equipping as many people as possible.

Broadcast Media

Millions of individuals experience *The Alternative with Dr. Tony Evans* through the daily radio broadcast playing on nearly 1,400 radio outlets and in over 130 countries. The broadcast can also be seen on several television networks and is available online at TonyEvans.org. You can also listen or view the daily broadcast by downloading the Tony Evans app for free in the App store. Over 30,000,000 message downloads/streams occur each year.

Leadership Training

The *Tony Evans Training Center* (TETC) facilitates a comprehensive discipleship platform which provides an educational program that embodies the ministry philosophy of Dr. Tony Evans as expressed through the kingdom agenda. The training courses focus on leadership development and discipleship in the following five tracks:

- Bible & Theology
- Personal Growth
- Family and Relationships
- Church Health and Leadership Development
- Society and Community Impact Strategies

The TETC program includes courses for both local and online students. Furthermore, TETC programming includes coursework for non-student attendees. Pastors, Christian leaders, and Christian laity, both local and at a distance, can seek out the Kingdom Agenda Certificate for personal, spiritual, and professional development. For more information, visit TonyEvansTraining.org.

The *Kingdom Agenda Pastors* (KAP) provides a *viable network* for *like-minded pastors* who embrace the kingdom agenda philosophy. Pastors have the opportunity to go deeper with Dr. Tony Evans as they are given greater biblical knowledge, practical applications, and resources to impact individuals, families, churches, and communities. KAP welcomes *senior and associate pastors* of all churches. KAP also offers an annual Summit held each year in Dallas with intensive seminars, workshops, and resources. For more information, visit KAFellowship.org.

Pastors' Wives Ministry, founded by the late Dr. Lois Evans, provides *counsel, encouragement,* and *spiritual resources* for pastors' wives as they serve with their husbands in the ministry. A primary focus of the ministry is the KAP Summit, which offers senior pastors' wives a safe place to *reflect, renew,* and *relax*, along with receiving training in personal development, spiritual growth, and care for their emotional and physical well-being. For more information, visit LoisEvans.org.

Kingdom Community Impact

The outreach programs of The Urban Alternative seek to provide positive impact to individuals, churches, families, and communities through a variety of ministries. We see these efforts as necessary to our calling as a ministry and essential to the communities we serve. With training on how to initiate and maintain programs to adopt schools, or provide homeless services, or partner toward unity and justice with the local police precincts (which creates a connection between the police and our community), we, as a ministry, live out God's kingdom agenda according to our *Kingdom Strategy for Community Transformation*.

The *Kingdom Strategy for Community Transformation* is a three-part plan that equips churches to have a positive impact on their communities for the kingdom of God. It also provides numerous practical suggestions for how this three-part plan can be implemented in your community, and it serves as a blueprint for unifying churches around the common goal of creating a better world for all of us. A course for this strategy is offered online through the Tony Evans Training Center at TonyEvansTraining.org/Courses/SCT.

Tony Evans Films ushers in positive life change through compelling video-shorts, animation, and feature-length films. We seek to build kingdom disciples through the power of story. We use a variety of platforms for viewer consumption and have over 120,000,000 digital views. We also merge video-shorts and film with relevant Bible study materials to bring people to the saving knowledge of Jesus Christ and to strengthen the body of Christ worldwide. *Tony Evans Films* released its first feature-length film, *Kingdom Men Rising*, in April 2019 in over 800 theaters nationwide, in partnership with Lifeway Films. The second release, *Journey with Jesus*, is in partnership with RightNow Media and was released in theaters in November 2021.

Resource Development

We are fostering lifelong learning partnerships with the people we serve by providing a variety of published materials. Dr. Evans has published more than 125 unique titles based on more than fifty years of preaching, whether that is in booklet, book, or Bible study format. He also holds the honor of writing and publishing the first full-Bible commentary and study Bible by an African American, released in 2019. This Bible sits in permanent display as a historic release in the Museum of the Bible in Washington, D.C.

For more information, and a complimentary copy of Dr. Evans's devotional newsletter, call (800) 800-3222 or write TUA at P.O. Box 4000, Dallas TX 75208, or visit us online at TonyEvans.org.

NOTES

1. Emily Russell, "'A Deep Depression after the Olympics.' The Challenges Facing Athletes at Home," NPR, February 20, 2022, https://www.npr.org/2022/02/20/1081945134/a-deep-depression-after-the-olympics-the-challenges-facing-athletes-at-home.
2. Dave Zangaro, "Torrey Smith 'Not Worried at All' about Living Up to Eagles' Expectations," *Philadelphia Inquirer*, December 7, 2017, http://www.nbcsports.com/philadelphia/eagles/torrey-smith-not-worried-all-about-living-eagles-expectations.
3. Ed Barkowitz, "Inside the Eagles' Nick Foles-to-Torrey Smith Flea-Flicker Touchdown Pass in the NFC Championship Game," *Philadelphia Inquirer*, January 22, 2018, https://www.inquirer.com/philly/sports/eagles/eagles-vikings-nfc-championship-flea-flicker-nick-foles-torrey-smith-sunday-night-20180122.html.

A KINGDOM EXPERIENCE FOR THE ENTIRE FAMILY!

Do you love *Kingdom Man, Kingdom Woman,* and other Kingdom books? Focus also offers a full selection of devotionals and curriculum in the Kingdom line. Devotions provide biblically sound encouragement to help you through each day. The group video experiences offer teaching from Dr. Tony Evans and participant's guides to help lead you toward a transformed life.

Get all of these great Kingdom products at
FocusOnTheFamily.com/Store

CP1555

THE KINGDOM SERIES
FROM DR. TONY EVANS

MORE RESOURCES TO GROW YOUR FAITH AND FURTHER GOD'S KINGDOM!

KINGDOM MAN
978-1-58997-685-6

KINGDOM MAN
DEVOTIONAL
978-1-62405-121-0

KINGDOM WOMAN
978-1-58997-743-3

KINGDOM WOMAN
DEVOTIONAL
978-1-62405-122-7

KINGDOM WOMAN
VIDEO STUDY
978-1-62405-209-5

KINGDOM MARRIAGE
978-1-58997-820-1

KINGDOM MARRIAGE
DEVOTIONAL
978-1-58997-856-0

KINGDOM MARRIAGE
VIDEO STUDY
978-1-58997-834-8

RAISING KINGDOM KIDS
978-1-58997-784-6

RAISING KINGDOM KIDS
DEVOTIONAL
978-1-62405-409-9

RAISING KINGDOM KIDS
VIDEO STUDY
978-1-62405-407-5

KINGDOM FAMILY
DEVOTIONAL
978-1-58997-855-3